Cape Breton
Book of the Night

Cape Breton

BOOK
OF THE

NIGHT

Stories of
Tenderness & Terror

EDITED BY RONALD CAPLAN

Breton Books
Wreck Cove
1991

ISBN 1-895415-08-X

Most of the stories in *Cape Breton Book of the Night* have
appeared in *Cape Breton's Magazine*.

Effie MacCorquodale Rankin transcribed the Gaelic for
Dan Angus Beaton's telling of "Raghnall Mac Ailein Oig"
and "Colainn gun Cheann." Paul Cranford transcribed the
pipe tune. Jocelyne Marchand taped, transcribed, and trans-
lated into English "Why Joe David Burned the House."
"Noel Morris's Encounter with the Devil" was retold in
Micmac and English by Bernie Francis.

Ronald Caplan has edited *Cape Breton's Magazine* since he
started it in 1972. He has edited two other books based on
the magazine: *Down North* (Breton Books, reprinted 1991)
and *Cape Breton Lives* (Breakwater Books, 1988).

Published by
Breton Books
Wreck Cove
Nova Scotia
B0C 1H0

Table of Contents

Editor's Introduction

AS IT HAPPENS, most of these stories were told to me at night. Often it was evening, just when we'd get to that part of our conversation where the give-and-take would give way to the sentences that connected for just one person, bringing up that person's story—and then one of us would fall silent and the other would talk.

I remember especially the night Art Severance told me the story about Truthful Paul. I had visited with Art before, looking for stories for *Cape Breton's Magazine*. We were comfortable with one another. Art liked those moments when conversation turned to stories. So far, this day had been one of conversation, mostly running over things we had talked about before—and all the time I just let the tape recorder run, turning the cassettes over when they stopped but not really looking for anything in particular. It was just Art and me and the tape recorder, and Sarah in the kitchen preparing an excellent supper. Not a bad day's work.

And I asked a question that made Art think of something I couldn't possibly have known to ask for. And then he leaned forward, elbows on knees and knees wide apart, his feet in slippers close together on the carpet, and he said, "I was storm-stayed Down North in 1928"— and I knew I was in for a story.

I deliberately didn't talk while he told the story, and the light kept falling, and neither of us dared stop to turn on the light, until the story was eventually finished in darkness. Truthful Paul.

•

This first collection of the *Cape Breton Book of the Night* is taken from stories collected for *Cape Breton's Magazine*; most of them have appeared as you find them here or as part of much longer life stories. In a sense, it has taken twenty years to gather these particular stories, only a few each year since the magazine started. They were not part of a project to collect unusual tales. Their form, and perhaps their generally humane telling, is probably the result of their coming up, usually without plan, in the midst of a conversation about a person's worklife or travels or interest in music or any of the subjects that appear in the magazine. In most cases, I was not particularly looking for a scary story. Conversely, I cannot remember a time when someone was trying to frighten me with these stories, at least not in any obvious way. It was something they shared with me, a part of their lives. And this, too, might explain the tone and timbre of these tales.

It should probably be added that some of them were stories the person was used to telling, stories that had been framed and honed. Others maintain the feel of a short piece of conversation. And some, such as Art's elegant telling of Truthful Paul and Bob Fitzgerald's account of the Big Fish are simply wonderful stories that may not have been told for years—stories that were triggered by our being together, perhaps by the extra importance *Cape Breton's Magazine* and a tape recorder brings to such a setting, some word or mood that brought the story to mind.

In all cases, I continue to be grateful for the arena *Cape Breton's Magazine* has created, the permission it has given me to be there to collect and then to transmit quickly back to the Cape Breton community the stories I have always considered nothing less than its own. This book, in a different form, is another portion of that continuing return.

•

And have I ever seen anything unusual? Only once. It happened at my home at Wreck Cove. I was waiting for a late night phone call and I didn't want to fall asleep. So I stretched out on the bed with my clothes on, crossed my hands on my chest and closed my eyes. Perhaps I fell asleep. I think I hovered somewhere in another kind of space, not quite asleep and not quite awake. In any case, the phone rang. I opened my eyes suddenly and looked at the corner of the room. There was a woman standing there, dressed in a kind of grey choir gown, from her shoulders to the floor. I think her hands were at her side. Her face had a kind of light greyness to it, almost like stone, and our eyes were locked on one another. She did not move. I was not afraid. And I am sure if I never took my eyes off her she would be standing there today. The phone rang again and, still looking at her, I moved to the phone. She did not move. I looked away for a second to pick up the receiver and when I looked back, she was gone. And I calmly reported into the phone what I had just seen.

Nothing has come out of it. Fr. John Angus Rankin felt it might be an important woman yet to come into my life. And I later learned that there was a woman who lived in that house, who had died young. But I have no explanation. It's not much of a story. But that's what happened to me.

Ronald Caplan
Wreck Cove
1991

What Angus Fraser Told about the Hairy Man

I DON'T SAY THERE IS ANYTHING THAT CAN'T BE EXPLAINED...well, I don't know. Except the hairy man, he lives down there (around Lowland Cove). I don't know. I didn't see him the last couple of years. But I've seen him previously.

(*Why do you call him the hairy man?*) Because he's got hair on him. He stands about eight feet, and he's got big arms that go down way beyond his knees. And he's got two picket ears, round eyes—nice beautiful round eyes—and that's about him. Long hair hanging down—like a great big fur coat. But I saw the eyes first. I sort of got fascinated with his eyes. There's about twenty people have seen him down there.

I met him at Wreck Cove (now Capstick) one night, me driving the half-ton truck—right in the centre of the road. Pretty near hit him. But he jumped. He jumped over the truck to get away from me hitting him. And I've seen him twice since then. I was in Meat Cove and then up in the Backlands. But I don't know what would he be. A crossbreed between humans and—what else?—the only explanation I have.

Lots of people have seen him. Years ago, too. The most that started him moving was when the mine was going. When they started blasting and drilling—then he started coming out. (*Did he ever hurt anybody?*) No. He'd stand just so close to me—and every time I'd move, he'd watch me, he'd follow me.

1

I was hunting in the woods one day, hunting deer. And he'd follow me. Like he was trying to study me, see what I was. And he followed for two miles in the woods—but he was staying far enough away so that I couldn't hurt him. I had the big gun in my hand—I could have fired at him any minute—but I know he wasn't going to hurt me.

He'd be as far from me as that boat. I'd stop behind a tree with a big deer gun, .303 in my hand. You know that's powerful. And he'd come close as that boat and he'd part the little alders that stand about eight feet. Part the alders, just looking at me. You could see his nice beautiful eyes. I call them beautiful eyes because they are so big. Long hair. The eyes are the first thing you'd notice. He'd look at me, wondering what I was, what I was doing. And then as soon as I'd move, the bushes would go together. He'd keep parallel with me—I was by the river coming out—till I got to the road. And I didn't see him any more.

(*Were you scared?*) I'm telling you I was scared. I didn't know what he was going to do. Was he supernatural or from outer space or something a bullet wouldn't hurt? I even lost respect for the gun, looking at him. But I wouldn't shoot because I thought then in my own mind that he could be half human. I imagine he was. I had the gun in my hand and could have shot him, but I thought back about what my uncle used to say about seeing him—which I thought then was some way to keep me in the house in the nighttime. But now I came to know it was true.

(*Do you think he's still living? Still out there?*) Yes. I have a feeling there's more than one of them there.

My grandfather, years and years ago, saw his track. He thought it was a bear's track and they followed it—from the Bear Mountain—for about four or five miles. That was spring of the year and

2

there was snow on the ground. But a bear doesn't walk on his hind legs that long. It would have to be him. Because his tracks were about six or seven feet apart, and it was like a man's foot. Of course, a bear's is, too—but no bear is going to walk on his two rear legs four or five miles. He came out of that Big Bear Mountain—that's the first place they discovered his track. There's one part of that Big Bear Mountain I don't believe anybody can get up to—it's sheer cliff. I don't think he could be there, but I always wanted to try to explore that area.

There were six together one night when they saw him. He was standing in the centre of the road. They were walking down from the mine. That's not too long ago. When he left them, he didn't turn his back on them. Just walked backwards into the woods. They went home and got the dog, see if they could track him down. Dog went as though it was a human being. Dog came back out.

Now I wouldn't be scared sleeping with him all night. Seems like he's harmless to anyone. But he's there. You set rabbit snares, or kill a deer, in the woods—and this happened to me so often it's not even funny. I'd put the deer up so high, if I was standing on your head I couldn't even reach it. When I came back, that deer was gone, it's taken. I mean, I could understand a bear's taking it or a wildcat eating it—but to get that it's got to be something more than a plain dumb animal.

For instance, there was an old windfall one time—me and a friend of mine, to protect the deer, we got a rope and worked it out, worked it out till we got it way out on the end of this limb—hauled the deer up. Whoever it was, came and opened the rope and let the deer down off the tree and took the deer. So help me God, no animal could have done that. Whoever he was, he opened those knots and took the deer, and no person would go out that far in the woods to do that. But it was taken and it had to be someone with a half-human brain.

3

Then another time I was stuck up beyond French River. There's a hill before you get to the last farm, before you start swinging right down to Lowland Cove—that was awful rough and hard to get out of. I went up there with the half-ton truck. And the road was just the width of the wheels. Whatever happened, I was going a little too fast and the ground was wet, and jumped over and the rear wheels were off the road—and I couldn't do anything unless I could get a machine to lift her back onto the road.

I took the gun out of the truck and walked up about another mile to Big Johnny's place—John Simon's father—over that field hunting for deer. Sat around, with the intention of later walking back out. But I felt I was neglecting the human race to leave my car there, with people with 4-wheel drives that might come and want to get past my truck.

When I came out, there was the truck, the rear end of the truck sitting right in the centre of the road. That's so help me God true. There was nobody else up there. There was an imprint—like a bear's imprint—right behind the car.

I've got a feeling this started way back—maybe somebody fired at him. And then when he came to me, inquisitive, and I didn't fire at him, maybe he got the idea he wanted to help me out. I know several times he was out in the woods, looking at me. I cut wood one day and I cut about four loads for a truck. But my back or arm was sore and I wasn't piling it—it was all spread over the ground. Way up at my father's old property. Okay. I went home, had dinner, I went back up— and it was all piled so nicely. Honest to God, I thought I'd shoot myself—this is crazy. There's no ten men could do it in that time. I just went back to Meat Cove for lunch and came back, and it was piled so nice, I could just lay it in the truck and bring it home. That was so beautiful.

4

Then another time I had rabbit snares. And if the rabbit is left on the ground for overnight and you don't come—the weasels—the young ones, you know—will eat at them, they're no good. You don't want to eat the rabbit if the weasel is going to begin on him. So I'd go out and all the rabbits would be hanging and the snares sort of set—not set like you'd set it or I'd set it—but sort of set. There was no sense in my having to check my snares unless I really wanted to, because they're not going to be on the ground.

People say they've seen the devil. Well, perhaps they've seen one of these creatures half-human, half-animal—perhaps they've seen the hairy man and they think it's the devil.

There were people hunting one night. And when they got to Sandy's field—they could see this thing going through the woods and down the road and stood there. Now a lady died a long time ago and buried some treasure there—or her brother buried treasure there—and everybody's been looking for it ever since. She had died years and years before. So these people were coming out from hunting; they were walking home. And when they turned the light on this thing going through the woods—I shouldn't say "thing" in case it's human—it stopped. They said it was a woman they saw, the woman whose property they were crossing—the story of the treasure made them think of the woman who had died. They described it as a woman with a big beautiful coat down to the ground. They said it was standing about eight feet tall. They couldn't see anything else, but they could see two great big eyes.

Amelia Cook: The Man Who Had Borrowed a Rope

AND THERE'S NEVER BEEN ONE SOUL to come back from the Beyond and tell us about it.

(Well, they seem to come back a lot on Cape Breton.)

Yes, but that's not the sort of thing they tell us. Not only that, they turn around and say, "I borrowed a rope...."

This man, they used to see him and see him and see him, and they were all scared of him. So one fellow said, "I'm going to speak to him." So this night they saw him and he spoke to him: "In the name of God, what do you want?"

"Well," he said, "I borrowed a rope from"— and he called his neighbour by name—"to take my cow to somebody's pasture, and I never gave it back. And the rope is hanging on the bars. It's bothering me. You give the rope back and you won't see me no more."

Sure enough they went, the rope was there. They gave it back and they never saw him again.

Dan MacNeil & the Devil, 1928

I DIDN'T SEE ANYTHING, BUT THIS THING
BOTHERED ME ON THE ROAD. That was in
1928. I was over to a wedding, and she was pretty
bad there, boy, they were fighting. They used to
fight like cats and dogs. Yes, those days, dances
and liquor, boy—they'd fight like cats and dogs.
They were monsters, they were big men, boy.
They'd fight. There'd be blood flying all over.
And I left there. It was dark as the devil in hell,
and I guess it was the devil that I met, too.

I started, boy, and I was going up a hill. And I
was just at the bottom of the hill. When I heard
this thing coming, coming down when I was going up, just like this, walking—like sheep walking. I thought it was sheep. This thing was coming towards me. And this thing just came, I'd
say, about ten or twelve feet and it slid right into
me and it made a sound like "bah."

I said to myself, That's only a sheep. Used to
be on the road those years.That's the kind of
sound it was. It didn't push me or anything. It
would come to six or seven or eight feet, and slide
right in. You've often seen a sheep bracing its
feet like this, forward—and this thing would
slide right in, and he'd make this queer noise.

My gosh, that was all right, that was the bottom of the hill, then. I thought it was only a
sheep, you know.

And then about halfways up the hill—you
wouldn't hear the thing going back at all—but
halfways up the hill, started again. The thing
coming towards me again, down the hill, boy.
And it came right about seven or eight feet to

you, and it slid in again, slid right in on the ground, and it made a "bah." Similar to a sheep, I'd say it was.

And then about top of the hill—it's the third time, boy. This thing started down towards me again. Going like this, boy, like a sheep. And it was maybe ten or twelve feet it slid in again—and slide on the ground. "Bah."

And I got mad, boy, I said, "You fly to Hell, you son-of-a-bitch!" I called him every name in the book. "You go straight to Hell," I said, "if it's you." Holy Christ Almighty, the racket he made going, boy, it was fearful. (*What kind of a racket?*) You'd think they were breaking fences and breaking sticks and everything else. That is the kind of a racket. The cove sounded. I never saw anything, but I heard this awful racket. And I'm pretty sure to this day, boy, it was the devil, trying to stop me.

It wasn't a sheep, I don't think; I don't think it was a sheep or a ram or anything. I think it was the old fellow himself. That's what I think. (*And it was a black night.*) Black as—it was kind of foggy, too, to make it worse. You couldn't see anything, what was coming. And you couldn't *hear* him going away from you—this is the funniest thing. But to hear it *come* to you.

And I'm pretty sure it was the devil. I was all alone. It was foggy and dark. Dark as a crow. It wasn't a sheep. It was trying to take me back to the dance. There might have been more trouble if I went back. And that's the only time in my life I ever met him. I didn't see anything, but whatever it was, I'm pretty sure it was him. Nobody else. I told that to lots of people and they say, "You're right. It was him, boy, trying to send you back over there."

(*Why do you think he came to you?*) Might have been more trouble if I went back. I don't know. I

8

was young then, spry. That's what I was thinking. That I'd get scared. Get into it over there. They were fighting at the wedding after that. I was thinking it was the old fellow himself.

It was no sheep. I took the beads out of my pocket, and I blessed myself. I used to wear a hat. I had lots of hair then, boy. My hat came right up over my head. By gosh, I was scared before I got home, but I said to him, "By gosh, there's not a devil in Hell that's going to stop me from going home."

He made quite a racket going. I called him all kinds of names, dirty names too, boy. I was mad.

Bob Fitzgerald & the Big Fish

YOU HEARD TELL OF THE BIG FISH— WINSTON, THAT'S BEFORE YOU WERE BORN. You know, the one that we harpooned. Captain Pearl was boss of the raft. *Winston Briand:* Gordon Dunphy told me about that one. *Bob Fitzgerald:* It was Gordon was the man that stuck him. *Winston:* Yes, the biggest mistake he ever made. *Bob:* Well, it was a tremendous big fish, you know—and he was going around here, and it was for days that we saw him. Why, he had a great dorsal fin on his back that high—oh, it was five or six feet high. He was an immense animal. Nobody'd ever go near him, didn't know what he was.

So Gordon was coming ashore from fishing— and Gordon had seen him. And Gordon went alongside of him in the boat, gasoline boat. So he was telling a bunch of us on the pier. He said,

9

"That's not a fish, that's the devil." "The devil?"
"Yes, it's the devil. I was up alongside of him today, and he's ninety feet long and he's got hair on
him." He said, "He's covered with hair." "Eh, go
on!" "Yes," he said, "he's got hair onto him—
that's what I took it to be anyway." Said, "I
didn't get too close to him. But he looked like he
had hair onto him."

Capt. Pearl was coming, walking out on the
wharf, heard us talking—came over. He listened
to the story. "By God, boys," he said, "we should
try and get her." "Try and *get* her?" "Yes," he
said, "we should try and get her." Old Capt.
Pearl, you know, he was an old sea dog, and he
was game for anything. And he had settled at
White Point. He had a house there.

"Well, okay. We'll try and get him, if there's
any use. Yeah."

He said, "We'll rig it up." So we got a sword-
fish dart and a piece of telephone wire and put it
through the dart—put about five feet of telephone
wire on it. And then we fastened a 21-thread hawser on it. Oh, I suppose sixty to seventy fathoms of
21-thread hawser. "Now, by Jesus," old Pearl said
now—"if we see him now—we'll give him a
twist."

That was in the morning. About three o'clock
in the evening, looked across the bay and there he
was. Somebody hollered, "There's the Big Fish!"
You could see him from White Point. Yes, he was
up about two miles or a mile and a half nor'west
of The Point—his great dorsal fin, man, stood as
high as this loft, six or seven feet. Looked like a
boat sail.

Now, I believe there were four boats. And we
were in John Will Dunphy's boat. John Will Dunphy fished there—had a big boat. And me and
Gordon and Capt. Pearl were in that one. I don't

10

remember if there was anyone else into her or not. But there were four boats in all. And Gordon was going to stick him.

So we leveled off for him and we were getting pretty close to him and Capt. Pearl wanted us to keep away, keep away—and we sneaked in onto him. And see, we were coming in on him kind of from his tail. His head was up here and we were coming in on him kind of slashways, this way—coming in for his big dorsal fin that was up now about four or five feet over the water. And I was standing up looking at him. I think there *was* hair on him. He was gray. But it couldn't be hair. It must've been something that looked like hair. But a terrible looking fish. My dear, I've seen plenty ugly fish, but that one, that fellow.... I'll swear that he was eighty feet long. He was the biggest beast ever I saw. He was a tremendous animal. I could see his head away way up, and there looked to be gills back about fifteen feet on his neck. Oh, he was out of this world. He was a tremendous, monstrous beast.

But we drifted in alongside of him anyway, very slowly—and Gordon come onto him. He drove his dart right down alongside of his big fin, right in those great sinews down alongside of his big fin, drove it in clean to the wood.

Well, as soon as he drove the dart in, the screeching took place—old Pearl yelling to start the engine. Anyway, we got clear, started playing out the rope. And the other fellows came. And the old fish didn't appear to take any notice of us too much. When we hit him, he started to settle away. And old Pearl yelled for everybody to string on. So we hooked the other three boats on.

See, with a 21-foot hawser and telephone wire into it, no darn way of breaking it—the devil wouldn't break it. And you'd never tear it out of him—not planted down the length of fourteen

11

inches of that iron down into him. No way. So we got three or four boats on him. And we started towing him towards the shore. The old fish coming along pretty good. No sign of him, you know. He had settled away. He was down under and we were moving him along, towards the shore. We were coming pretty good. Coming along, and old Pearl—he's hollering to "Speed her up! Give her a little more!" So all hands speeded the engines up a little, and we were taking him along pretty nice. Not bad at all.

But you know, we were getting in pretty well—we were in off of the Tittles. *Winston:* That's shallow water. *Bob:* And all of a sudden that fish decided that he was going to go the other way. He decided that he was far enough in. And one minute we were going along. And the next minute we were going the opposite way. All four boats. That fish—he started out for deep water. And we were nothing behind him, the same as we were only a feather behind him. And he straightened away. And I'll tell you that he started to make things hum. And he was putting on speed. And the other fellows decided it was time to chop clear. And outside, the two fellows behind chopped away. And we started to screech. I was screeching to Gordon to cut him clear, and somebody looked for a knife and we couldn't find one. And that rope was tied to a thwart—you know, the plank seat across the boat—and he ripped it clear and took part of the engine house—but it ripped out and the end of it hooked under the stern as it was going. Hooked where it was decked over. And boy, the water was starting to fly over us, and I said to myself, "We're going down."

And Gordon jumped. He seized a hatchet. There was a hatchet by him—and he made a swipe at that rope to cut it off, that rope going out over the stern—and he missed it. And I thought to myself he would never have time for to have another swipe at it. And the water was flying over

12

us, clean over us, and old Pearl was screeching and everybody was yelling, and Gordon went over his head once more and took one swipe at that, and that time he hit it. And boy, if he hadn't chopped that rope clear, we were going down.

And we were doing about eighteen or twenty knots steaming, and the water flying over us—and when he chopped the rope, we stopped so sudden that I went end over end, and there was one boat still fastened onto us and he came smashing into us. And I'm telling you, my friend, that it was a good job that he got that rope chopped off. Or if he didn't, I don't think that I'd be telling you the story tonight.

Because I think we would have gone down that night and that would have been it. Because that fish—we were nothing at all behind him. He just went on. He didn't mind those four boats behind him. He didn't mind those four boats behind him any more than.... That thing was eighty feet long, man. That thing would weigh twenty-five tons. He didn't *know* that there was anything behind him.

(*And what was it?*) Well, I'll tell you. It may have been a shark—I've never seen a shark like it, and I've seen sharks off here 40 feet long. I was telling Alexander Dunphy—he fished on the Grand Banks many years—and he said he saw those fish down among the Virgin Rocks in the spring of the year, southeast corner of the Grand Banks. I forget what he called them now.

(*But Bob, why go after that creature at all—he was no use to you.*) Well, you know, a fisherman is like that. Oh, yes. A fisherman has got that streak of hellery in him. If he sees a fish, it doesn't make any difference, he'll try to get him. There's a certain amount of deviltry in everybody. And a little adventure.

13

Mary Sarah MacNeil & Lights

(MARY SARAH, I THINK OF PLACES LIKE LONG ISLAND AS BEING SO SOLITARY, you know, and people often tell me about experiences that they had, either religious, or seeing people who have died. At Long Island, was there ever...?) Connection with the dead. No, no. (*Or spiritual feeling.*) No, no. Not a thing.

But we heard a lot of ghost stories and things like that—an old man riding on a stove, coasting on a stove down to the shore. And the man that picked up the bracelet that the devil lost. And this old lady used to tell a story that there'd be a fire on top of the house, and a fire on top of the barn, and the two of them would come over and hit against one another above the road. And they'd go in sparks up. After awhile, they'd come back again on top of the barn, on top of the house, they'd come back, hit against, and go in sparks in the middle—halfways between the house and the barn. We heard those stories, but that's only stories....

I told you there wasn't anything spooky about it, but there was. There was a young fellow over there—as a matter of fact, he's still living—but not on the island—a Nicholson fellow. A light used to follow him. But that was true. Different people saw the light following him.

He was at our place one night. You know, he used to live right across the field from our place, and there was a line fence between them. He was at our place one night, him and his sister. And they were going home. A light came across from Boularderie, over to where they were. He said to her, "Look at that light." And she couldn't see anything. And he said he put his hands on his face, and he could see the light through his fingers—and she couldn't see it at all.

Then when they'd have to climb over the fence. If he was going to climb it, he'd go on this side of her, he was holding onto her. He was scaring the life out of her. He'd go on her right side, and the light would come and go on his side of the fence. And when he'd go on the other side of her, the light would go on the other side. She never saw the light. And they got home, and they fell on the floor, in the kitchen, in the house. They almost— well, he scared the life out of her. And he was scared because he was seeing the light.

Then there was another night, there used to be a butcher come, and his name was Millen. He used to come up and get orders, whoever had lambs or sheep or anything to sell. And he'd stay at this Nicholson house. This night, Millen was at the house, and my Uncle Dan was there, and Malcolm Nicholson in the other house was there. And they told this same fellow to go down to the barn to get a bucket of coal. So he went to the barn, and after awhile he fell in on the floor, and he said the light was after him.

So they all went out. And they all saw the light. The light was going back over—it went over to Boularderie, and it started going up above Boularderie. Then the fellow came out to the door. As soon as he came out to the door, it stopped, and it started coming back. The fellow went back in again. Now that was true, because my uncle saw the light. But the night he was with his sister, his sister couldn't see the light. But he did.

But that light was after him different times, in the nighttime. That light would come. But that night that the crowd was with him, he should have stayed out with them that night, and let the light come back, see what would it do. Because, it

wouldn't harm him with all the others with him.
When it wouldn't harm him with his sister with
him, it wouldn't harm him with the others. So he
should have—that's what everybody was saying,
he should have stayed out. But he was too scared.
As soon as he went back in again, the light started
back again. They watched it, and they said it went
all up over Boularderie, right out of sight. He saw
it different times after that.

(*But he never found out just what the light was?*)
No, never found out what it meant, what it was or
what it meant, or anything. He's still living. But I
think he got rid of that light quite a number of
years ago. It quit bothering him, whatever it was.
But it was a true—it was true. 'Cause different
people saw it. (*You yourself, you didn't.*) No, I never saw it, no, I never. No, I never saw anything or
heard anything.

Donald John MacMullin & a Man Called "The Pig"

THERE WAS A MAN CALLED THE PIG, and a good many people would think it wasn't a nice name but it was. My grandfather told me the story.

This man had a big black dog, according to my grandfather. He knew him well. And the dog would never pay no attention to nobody. He'd look at you. Wouldn't growl or nothing.

But the man went fishing this night, fishing for salmon or something, spearing. We did that here. You know, spear salmon with a light. And he saw a light ahead of him around a turn, and he came up with a stranger. The stranger said, "You're fishing?" The man says, "Yes." "Well," he says, "why can't we fish together?" "Well," the man says, "I might think that over." "Oh, yes," the stranger says, "we can divide the fish, one to you and one to me and," he says, "the last big one for me."

The man caught on he had the wrong man with him.

So they start fishing. And soon the stranger says, "We've got enough." "Oh, no," says the man, "there's lots of fish in the brook yet."

You see, I have an idea or two—that's why I like the rooster. If the rooster crows at any bad persons in the olden times, you were gonna know. So, he was killing time. And the pheasant rooster—out of a clear sky—the pheasant rooster crowed in the woods alongside of him. He said, "I've got to go. We'll have to divide the fish."

They started dividing the fish and the man started measuring them, even lengths—but he didn't agree with giving him the big fish, the last one, at all. So, anyhow, the big fellow went. He said, "Only for your trickery, we should have this division long ago."

And all right, the dog never moved.

Coming home, there was a big black pig met them, and she charged the man. I guess his shoes weren't too good. He kicked her and kicked her and the shoes went off his feet. But the dog came to life and charged into the black pig. And the dog and the pig went at it and they went out in the water. And nobody ever saw one of them since.

The dog went. The pig went. But the man came to Cape Breton. And he was always called Muiceadh—The Pig.

Dan Angus Beaton Tells about Raghnall Mac Ailein Oig

(English begins on page 23)

(English begins on page 23)

NAIDHEACHD AIG AN FHEAR A BHA 'G EU-GHACHD AIR ANNS A' CHLADH, da cheud bliadhna mun do rugadh e. Bha leithid de dhuine ann, fear ris an abradh iad Raghnall Mac Ailein Oig. Bha cladh thall ann an Albainn agus bha guth ag eughachd air anns a' chladh, da cheud bliadhna mun do rugadh e riamh. Leis an sin, dh'fhalbh daoine as an àite, cha robh iad a' fuireach mu chuairt ann idir—chaidh fhàgail uile.

Raghnall Mac Ailein Oig a bha seo—'se Mac-Leoid a bh'ann dar a rugadh e. Ach mu dhei-readh thall, bha teaghlach de MhacLeoid ann an Albainn anns an robh dà Ailean—Seann Ailein is Ailean Og. Dar a thainig Ailean Og gu aois—phòs e. An deidh beagan bhliadhnaichean bha mac aige. Nuair a bha mac là neo dha dh'aois chaidh falbh leis gu bhi air a bhaisteadh agus bha'n eaglais suas ri fichead mìle air falbh.

An deidh dhaibh falbh, thainig seann choim-hearsnach a dh'ionnsaidh an tighe a choimhead air an fhear òg a rugadh agus dh'fhoighneachd e airson an leanabh. Thuirt iad ris, "Tha iad an deidh falbh leis gu bhi air a bhaisteadh." "An e gille neo nighean a th'ann?" "O, 'se gille th'ann." "De'n t-ainm a thug sibh air?" "'Se Raghnall a thug sinn air." "O, an ainm an fhortain," thuirt e, "do chuimhnich sibh idir, sin ainm an fhir air an robhar ag eughach anns a' chladh bho chionn da cheud bliadhna."

Thug athair cruinn leum as—"Airson Dia, cha do studaig mise riamh air. Feumar stad a chur

19

air a' bhaisteadh agus air an ainm, ma ghabhas e idir," agus mach a ghabh e. Leum e air muin each eile bha anns an t-sabhal agus start e aig cruaidh ghalap as deidh an fheadhainn a dh'fhalbh. A dh'aindeoin na rinn e ghalap 'sa dh'fhalbh, dar a rainig e an eaglais—bha am baisteadh seachad. Thuirt e ris an t-sagart, "Feumar an t-ainm seo bhi air a sheingeadh, chan fhaod e bhith." Thuirt iad ris, "Cha ghabh an t-ainm a bhi air a sheingeadh a nis, seo an t-ainm a bhios air gus am bi e marbh." Cha ghabhadh sian deanamh tuilleadh— bha Raghnall Mac Ailein Oig ann mu dheireadh.

Cha robh fios aig athair de dheanadh e, bha'm fear beag a' startadh air fàs. "Rud is fhearr dhomhsa dheanamh, 'se'n t-àite seo fhàgail uile gu leir, far nach cluinn an gille gu bràth gun robhar ag eughach air agus gun d'thug mise'n t-ainm." Dh'fhalbh e 's chaidh e cros gu taobh eile dh'Albainn uile gu leir. Ach bha'n gille fàs agus bha e ainmeil ainmeil uile tapaidh anns an sgoil ann an ionnsachadh agus cha robh e fad's am bith gus an robh e na dhuine. An deidh dha sgoil fhàgail, chaidh e shèoladh—'se soithichean siùil a bh'ann uile an uair ud. Cha robh e fad sam bith gus an d'fhuair e bhi na chaiptean, a' seoladh bho eilein gu eilein, bho àite gu àite.

Bha da sheann duine comh' ris air an t-soitheach air an robh e agus bha e seoladh gu ruige Eilein Leodhais, na gu bith caite'n robh e dol agus rug stoirm uamhasach orra mu dhorchadh na h-oidhche.

Agus thuirt e ris an fheadhainn a bha comh' ris, "Feumaidh sinn a dhol astigh gu acarsaid an seo—chan urainn dhuinn cuir suas ris an stoirm." "O," thuirt an seann duine ris, "na teid astigh an sin idir, idir, idir, ni sinn an ath acarsaid dheth." "Carson?" ars esan. "Mas urainn dhuit, na teid astigh an sin idir, 's fhearr dhuit an ath acarsaid a dheanamh dheth." "Is mise ceannard an t-soithich, 's tha mi dol astigh."

20

Se sin a bh'ann—chaidh iad astigh. Bha e gu math dorcha agus leig iad sios an acair an seo. Cha robh iad ach air an acair a leagail sìos dar a chual e bhi 'g eughach air. Thionndaidh e 's thuirt e ri luchd a bhàta, "Co fo'n Ni tha 'g eughachd ormsa, neo co aig tha fios gur mise thainig astigh an seo?" Thionndaidh an seann fhear agus dh'innis e dha, "Tha'n guth sin anns a' chladh air a bhi 'g eughachd ortsa bho chionn da cheud bliadhna mun do rugadh tu riamh."

"Ma tha sin mar sin," thuirt esan, "chan urainn nach eil feum mór aig orm. Thig sinn gu tir agus thig dithis na triuir comh' riumsa agus thig sinn far a bheil e."

Leig iad sios am bata beag ach thainig an guth as a' chladh, "A Raghnaill 'ic Ailein Oig, thig an seo leat fhein agus thoir leat do chlaidheamh." "Seall sin a nis," thuirt an seann fhear, "tha thu faicinn nach tig thu as gu brath ma theid thu ann." "Biodh sin mar a bhitheas e, tha mise dol ann," thuirt esan.

Leum e anns a' bhata 's thug e leis an claidheamh 's dh'fhalbh e anns an dubh dall dorcha mar a bha i. Chaidh e air tir 's chitheadh e beagan de'n ghealaich an drasda 'sa rithis a' tighinn ris. Cha deanadh e rathad troimh'n choille 'son droighneach a bh'ann. Bha mu mhìle gu leth neo da mhìle aige ri dhol anns an uamharraidh bha sin gus an d'thainig e gu seorsa de chlearadh a bh'anns a' choille. De bha stigh an sin ach cladh beag.

Dar a thainig e teann air a' chladh, chunnaic e corp duine stobadh amach gu mheadhoin as a' chladh—chum e direach a null far an robh e 's thuirt e ris, "Tha theannsa gur tusa tha g' eughach ormsa?" "'S mi," ars esan. "Tha mi 'g eughachd ort o chionn da cheud bliadhna." "Carson mis' seach duine sam bith eile?" "A chionns gu robh fhios agam nach robh duin' eile air an t-saoghal aig an robh mhisneachd a thigeadh an seo ach thu fhein." "Well, well," fhreagair e, "chan urainn nach eil feum sònraichte agad ormsa."

"Tha," thuirt esan, "tha. Dar a bha mis' òg bha mi falbh comh' ri nighean òg 's gheall mi dhith gun cumainn mo ghealltanas ged a chaillinn an ceann far na gualainn. Cha do chum mise mo ghealltanas idir. Chan fhan mise stigh san àite mhór tha thall gus an caill mi'n ceann far na gualainn. Cha bhi tamhachd dhomhsa anns an t-saoghal thall gus an éirich dhomhsa mar a gheall mi. Rud tha agads' ri dheanamh, 'se'n ceann a chuir dhiomsa leis a' chlaidheamh a th'agad an sin."

"Ni mise sin dhuit mas e sin tha dhith ort." "Dar a ni thu e," ars esan, "fagaidh tu an claidheamh na laighe air m'amhaich gus an fhuaraich an fhuil 's cha chluinn 's chan fhaic duine mise gu bràth tuilleadh."

Thog Raghnall Mac Ailein Oig gu h-ard an claidheamh 's le aon swing, bha'n ceann dheth. Dh'fhag e'n claidheamh air an amhaich gus an do dh'fhuaraich an fhuil, sguir a' bhruidhinn 'sa fuaim 's chan fhac e sian tuilleadh.

Bha'n fheadhainn air a' bhàta deanamh deiseal gu falbh—cha robh dùil aca gu faiceadh iad Raghnall gu bràth tuilleadh, ach chunnaic iad a' tighinn e 's chaidh e air a' bhàta: agus theirig an eughach agus theirig an naidheachd, agus sin agad e.

Dan Angus, in English:

RAGHNALL MAC AILEIN OIG—he stopped a lot of crime over in Scotland in the old days, you know. He was a noted man in Scotland in the old times. He was a tremendous strong man. He was one of the ablest men that Scotland ever produced, you know, a MacLeod. An awful lot of stories about Raghnall Mac Ailein Oig, not one or two or three or four—there's lots of stories about Raghnall Mac Ailein Oig.

How he defeated the Headless Woman in the cave, and how that came about. That was one. There's even a tune. You know, where she lived in that cave—there were hundreds of bodies and brains and heads and skulls in there where she killed them. And he did away with that.

And how he got there in the first place. You heard when he was called for in the graveyard 200 years before he was born? This is the last one I'll tell you. There are too many about him. But I'll give you this one, and this is the last one.

Raghnall Mac Ailein Oig—he was Young Allan's son—Ailean Og—Ronald Young Allan—you understand me? Okay, now I'll tell it in English, but it was all in Gaelic.

There was a family in Scotland. Well, there was a graveyard in Scotland. And for years there was a voice calling in it for a man by the name of Ronald Young Allan, Raghnall Mac Ailein Oig, to come there, that he wanted him. And my God, there was no such a man in Scotland. And this voice was calling for Ronald Young Allan for 200 years before he was born. With the result that people didn't want to live near that graveyard, they kind of moved away from it. Do you understand it? Hearing this voice at night, calling, the graveyard. People didn't want property even near it. Their land became kind of more or less vacant and not want-

23

ed. So for years and years, people kind of stayed away from the place. There was no such a man.

But there was a place then, there was a family there, and there was an Allan in it. And then, by golly, there was another Allan in it—there were two Allans. Nobody ever thought anything of that. But this Young Allan got married. And there was an old man in the community. After Young Allan was married for awhile, a son was born. So (the old man) went to the home to see how the young baby was coming. He went into the house. And he said he'd like to see the new baby. "Oh, he's sent to be baptized." "Oh, it's a boy, eh?" "Yes." "And what do you call him?" "We call him Raghnall." "Oh, my God," the old fellow said, "do you people realize that that's the man they've been calling for in the graveyard since over 200 years?" The (grand)father thought. "My God, that would be Ronald, Young Allan's son."

So he just didn't hesitate, he made for the barn. The couple had left on horseback with the child to be baptized at the church. They were gone about an hour. The church was a long distance off. So he took off after them with another team—he'd catch them and stop it, change the name. But by the time they got to the church, they were just through—he was baptized. "Oh," he said, "you've got to change that name." They said, "It cannot be done. Baptized and named," he said, "and it cannot be changed. He's Raghnall MacLeoid, Raghnall Mac Ailein Oig. That's it."

So as he was growing, the father said, "This is awful. What am I going to do? That child, now, he'll grow up, and he'll hear this, and maybe go crazy over it." He said, "I'd better get out of here." So he moved clear across Scotland altogether, so the child would never hear of it.

He was a very brilliant child. Smart in school. Strong. Exceptionally strong boy. Took up sailing.

He wasn't long sailing when he became a captain. In those days it was all sailboats. There were no steamboats or anything like that. No powerboats. All sail, you know. He took up sailing. He wasn't long sailing when he became a captain.

And he was going across some cove, going from island to island—I guess there's a lot of islands over there to go to, and places to go to with different cargo. By golly, he was out this certain night, this certain trip, and got caught in an awful storm. But he had a couple of old fellows with him, particularly this one old fellow on the boat with him, that knew about him, that he was the man that the voices were calling for. And it happened that they were having to go by not too far from this place. But they got caught in this awful storm.

"Well," he says, "we've got to go into port. We can't live this storm out." "Oh," this old fellow said to him, "no," he says, "we can't go into this port." He says, "There's an old harbour here. We'll have to go into it." "Oh, no, no, Captain," he says, "keep going. We can make the next harbour of it." He knew about this voice being in there, you know. He says, "I'm captain, and I know what I'm doing." "Don't go into this port," the old fellow told him. "Try and make the next one of it." "Why? I'm going in here," he said. "I'm in charge."

Well, there was nothing more said. He went in. They landed shortly before midnight in the harbour, and put down anchor. And, God, they had no sooner anchored when he heard being called— the voice in the graveyard calling him. He turned to the crew and he said, "My God," he said, "who would know that I even came in here? (Who would) know my name?" And this old fellow came up and told him, "That's why I didn't want you to come in here. That voice has been calling for you 200 years before you were born. For God's sake, don't go near that. Stay away from it."

"Well, well," he said, "now, if that voice has been calling for me before I was born, and especially 200 years before I was born, he must desperately need me." So he said, "Put one of the boats over, we're going ashore. And so many of you are going with me." "No way, we don't want to go with you!" "You're coming with me," he said, "we're going. And going into that graveyard."

So after they lowered the boat over, the voice hollered, "Ronald Young Allan, come all alone. And take your sword." All by himself. Didn't want anybody else. Old fellow told him, "Look, what'd I tell you? Are you foolish enough now to go in there?" "Well," he said, "so be it. I'm going. He must need me worse than I need him. So," he says, "I'm going. Needs me for some reason, if he's been calling for over 200 years. I'm going." Put the boat over, and he left. "Well," (the old man) says, "we'll never see that man again."

So he left, and he went over, and he went ashore. Once he got ashore in that young spruce and sage and stuff that was there, he pulled the boat ashore. He left. He had to go about a mile or a half through that awful wilderness, travelling. The moon would now and then show through the clouds as he was making his way to the graveyard, carrying his sword with him. There were no flashlights or any lights in those days—nothing. He finally was getting closer and closer to the voice. At last he came into a little clearing—the graveyard. He got over, right to where the voice was.

And here was the body of a man sticking out of the grave, about that much. Up to his waist. Sticking out of the grave.

Well. He told him who he was. And Ronald said to him, "They tell me that you were calling for me for over 200 years." He says, "Yes. I have." "Why me?" "Because I knew that you'd be the only man that would have the courage to come here and do what I want done." Now. Yes. "What is it you want done?"

"Raghnall," he said, "I'll tell you. When I was a young man, I was going with a girl. And I gave her a death promise, a life promise, that I'd lose my head from my shoulders before I'd break it." He said, "And I didn't keep that promise to her. I cannot get rest in the other world until this happens. I've got to lose the head from the shoulders before I can get in there, have rest in the other world. Now what I want you to do is to take your sword," he says, "and chop my head off. And when you do, leave the sword lay on my neck till the blood gets cold. Now when you do that, you'll hear my voice no more."

"Well," Ronald said, "if that's all you want done, I'll oblige you." And he took the sword and he swung her, and *off* comes the head. And he let the sword lay on the neck until the blood did get cold. And they never heard the voice no more.

And the fellows on board ship were saying, "We'll never see that man." And they were wondering who was going to take the ship out after the weather would calm down. When, the first thing they knew, he was coming back and going aboard. And that's the end of that story.

Johnny "Cook" MacDonald

I CAN'T EXPLAIN IT (*Johnny "Cook" told us at Skir Dhu*). But it's running in people. That's it. My uncle used to—when he was living over in the old house—he'd have some of the tools hanging up, you know, in the end of the house—and his room was at the opposite end. And he told me, "Many's the night," he said, "that I had to get up and take them tools off the nail and put them out of my sight. They were all lit up." And these are the tools he was using to make coffins....

I went up to the post office one night. It was the old road then. Narrow road. Just something like what's going down to the shore here. And right up at the schoolhouse, I thought I heard something, behind me. And I was just stepping off the road, you know, going up towards Tommy's, to go over to D.J.'s to the post office—and I saw a horse and a sleigh. A grey horse and one man sitting on the sleigh. And it went by and it went about 100 feet beyond where I was . And I looked and here was another horse coming down this way. A white horse. And the whole thing, you know, changing something from one sleigh to the other, only took seconds. The white horse was facing down this way, just in a flash. And the other horse was facing up the other way, in a flash. And the whole thing went out of my sight right there.

And that came to pass. Two months after that, Neilie Shaw, he was killed out in Cobalt, Ontario—and they took his remains home in March. And that's how they took him home. There was somebody met the remains at Englishtown. They took him so far. And Donny Plaster took them from his place till he met Sandy Kenny's father up at the schoolhouse here. And Sandy Kenny's father took the remains down to the Shaws. Now I saw that as plain as day.

But do you know what? I got scared. The first time I ever got scared of anything like that. It was kind of a dark night and I was pretty darned scared coming home. I was never scared out at night—seeing things, you know, like that—but I was scared that night.

28

Kate Redmond on St. Paul's Island

PEOPLE USED TO TELL STORIES OF PEO-
PLE WHO DIED ON ST. PAUL'S. You see, if
you died there you had to wait until summertime
to be buried. And there were stories—I don't
know if my older sister made them up—that
there were money-hunters and they'd dig them
up and take the rings off people's hands.

There was a funny thing happened when I was
very young. I had a younger sister, Marie. She
was a very beautiful child. She had golden hair
and the most beautiful eyes you ever saw. She
looked like an angel. We all sort of worshipped
her. Some people told my mother she would never raise her, she was too beautiful. Anyway, she
did live, although she was the only one of the
family that died.

But anyway, I remember this night. The
night—the moon would shine, you could see the
pictures on the wall in the bedroom. It seemed
like a brighter moon than we get here. And we
were in this great big bedroom. My older sister,
Caroline, she slept in one corner. My bed was
over in the other corner. And I had my sister
Marie with me.

And during the night, I felt like there was
something in bed with us. And my sister Marie
was on the inside, next to the wall. And this thing
pushed against Marie and I got over to the edge
of the bed and pulled Marie over by me and it
kept pressing. And I put my foot down and it was
like a hairy leg.

And I'd look around the room and I could see
the sky and the pictures on the wall. And I'd

whisper "Caroline, Caroline"—and every time I would say anything this thing would press harder. I was scared to get out of bed, this thing would jump and catch me. But I was wide awake. And I could hear him breathing. Queer heavy low breathing.

So anyway I put through the night. When I heard Mama moving down in the kitchen, I beat it downstairs. I told Mama. And she moved my bed. "Oh," she said, "I think you were just imagining."

But years afterward, I asked her why she moved it if she didn't believe. "Well," she said, "there were bad things happened there. And who knows but what some spirit was earthbound."

That was my only experience. But it was so real that I can feel it, feel the shinbone. The hair on whatever it was legs.

When Fr. John Angus Rankin Saw His Father

WELL, IT WAS MY EXPERIENCE WITH MY FATHER THAT REALLY CONVINCED ME THAT PEOPLE CAME BACK. Because I had certain criteria. Number One, I had to be in full possession of my faculties. Number Two, the person had to be dead. And Number Three, I had no way of knowing what was in his mind, or her mind. Now, if I got a situation where those three conditions were fulfilled simultaneously, I wouldn't doubt.

(*Did you know your father was going to die, before he died?*) Yes, yeah. (*What gave you that information?*) Oh, it was more a forerunner—it was a premonition, see. Coming into the house, and the house was in darkness. And the parlour was lit up. And I figured, well, maybe somebody got into the back door. But as soon—I had my own key for the house—as soon as I unlocked the door and went in, I was in complete darkness. (*How did the parlour figure?*) Well, that's where the wake was held. So it was something along the idea of the light I was talking about, eh? Saw the place, saw the room lit up.

(*Did your father die suddenly?*) No, he was sick for about a week. And see, I was teaching down at the college at the time. And I was down, oh, every day. I stayed down Thursday night and went back and taught classes all day Friday. I was going to stay home Friday night in Antigonish. But the phone rang at six o'clock that he'd taken a very serious turn and gone unconscious. So I came right back down. And he died at one o'clock in the morning.

So after the funeral was over, I knew where he dealt, the people he dealt with in Inverness. So I went to the Town Hall, for taxes, 'cause he died in April. And half the tax bill was paid, so I paid off the rest—got a receipt. He dealt with the Co-op store. I went there, and there was nothing there. He joined the Co-op after he had been a long-time member of a local merchant's store—he and the merchant were great friends. So I went there, and all that was owing was the current bill. So I paid that. And I said, "Let's look back." He said, "Your father always paid his bill." "Let's go back so many years." He looked back—nothing.

So I knew then that everything was paid for. As far as I was concerned, there were no debts. Because those were the three places that he could have had something, and he had two—some of the taxes and some of the current bill.

He died in April. The following. I came home once or twice, and the house in darkness, like it was the night I saw the light. And one night I was shaving in the kitchen. And I could swear that I heard the front door opening, and somebody walking in. There was only a light on in the kitchen. So I dropped the razor, and went through. Eerie feeling. But nothing—doors locked, and everything else. My mother and my uncle, who was staying with her, came in later. But I didn't say a word to them, because I didn't want to scare them.

Then on another occasion I came home. And he had a favourite place to sit—we had a sun porch. And he could sit in the front of the sun porch and put his face like this and watch everything going on up the street. Opened the gate and came in. And I was sure I saw him. So sure that I didn't go in the house at all. I went over to the neighbour's and stayed there till the folks came home. (*You thought you saw your father.*) I thought I saw him. But I didn't go in.

32

Then that summer, the summer after he died, I was teaching down at Xavier Junior College in Sydney. I was staying at Point Edward. And it was just about the—almost the end of the term of summer school. So all the students were doing was reviewing, and I didn't have to prepare a class for the next day.

So, Joe MacLean and I were great friends. So after supper I went over to Joe MacLean's, and we got into music. And Joe played music with me, I suppose, from eight till about midnight or so. I drove back to the staff house at Coxheath. And Dr. MacLellan was up watching an old show about the English mines—I forget the name of it now. But anyway, he left me. He said, "I'm getting too tired." And I had never seen this show, but being a miner's son, I wanted to see....

The show was over, I'd say, about 1:30. So I had to go upstairs. And MacLellan said, "Be sure and put off the lights when you leave." I snapped off the TV, snapped off the light in the parlour, and walked up the stairs.

And my bedroom was down—there's a corridor, a long hall going down—it was the last room. And I knew the place so bloody well. I snapped off the centre light here. I was in semi-darkness. And I walked down the length of the corridor to my room. And all I had to do was reach in and get the switch. I had music books that Joe MacLean gave me in my hand. So I was thinking of tunes that Joe had played.

I snapped on the light, and my father was standing on the other side of the bed. I could see him from the knees up. And the only difference was, when he was in the casket, the undertaker, who knew him, combed his hair the way he used to comb it when he was younger, parted on the side here and all pulled over. As my father got older, the hair got thinner here, so he used to part

33

it down the centre and put it this way. That's the way his hair was combed when I saw him standing at the bed. So I got a shock.

And I said, "What do you want? What's the matter?" And then, before he would have said anything, I said, "Are you saved?" He said, "Yes, you know I'd be saved."

And then I said again, "What do you want?" He said, "A bill." "Oh," I said, "no, there isn't." He said, "Yes, there is." I said, "Where?" He said, "Malcolm Dan MacLellan's. $16.25. And," he said, "the bill is 25 years old."

By this time, I had lost my fear. And I turned my eyes off him, because I was getting ready to ask questions about the other world. I put the book down on the table, and turned. There was nothing there. (*Oh, he didn't stay and talk to you.*) No. As soon as he got the message across, he disappeared.

Well, I didn't sleep all night. I just sat there and smoked cigarettes. Dawn came, I went out and said Mass. So then I went to see MacLellan, and I told MacLellan. And I said, "I had an awful experience last night." I said, "I don't believe in this." I said, "There's only one other case quite similar. I'm going to go to Inverness and," I said, "if there's a bill in Inverness, then I've got to believe it. If not," I said, "I'm going on to Halifax to see a psychiatrist." So it was a Saturday morning. He said, "Go ahead."

So I came home, and I went over to the merchant. And I called him aside. And I told him what happened. "No, no, no," he said, "no, no. Your father is even." "Well," I said, "there's something. I'd like to—have you got old bills?" "Oh," he said, "well, yeah, yeah, yeah." "Well," I said, "I want to go through them." He said, "Wait a minute. I'm kind of busy now. But at dinnertime there'll be a lull. I'll go with you."

34

So he took me upstairs to an old office he had, and we went through every bloody bill—no, nothing. So he said, "Look at that!" He said, "Your father would come up from the mine, after working all day. And I'd have hay out. And," he said, "he'd come over. I'd come after him. And he'd go over and he'd put in hay with me till I got all the hay in." He said, "I owe *him* something."

"Well," I said, "if I don't get that bill, I'm going to go to Halifax. Because you told me the bills were paid, and I have no way of knowing."

So we were arguing back and forth, and going through bills, and the son came along. And he said, "What's going on?" So his father, "Well, Fr. John here," he said, "is looking for an old bill. And he figures his father owes some money to the store. And there's no...." "Oh, Dad," he says, "remember the boxes you gave me the other day?" He said, "There were old bills in there—you told me to burn them." He said, "I didn't get a chance to burn them. There's old bills there—they go back a long time."

Third bill down! A ton of—we used to have a cow in Inverness—a ton of hay my father got. One ton of hay—$16.25 for a ton of hay then. So, he didn't want—I said, "No, here." I said, "You're taking the bloody money. You do with it what you wish. Give me that bloody bill." And in the presence of them, I burned the bill and gave him the money.

My brother, my younger brother, was going to the seminary at the same time, and he used to go over to Malcolm. Malcolm would give him $5, $10 sometimes. This evening he went over to get some groceries. Malcolm gave him the $16.25! He came home. He said, "I don't know what in the name of God is wrong with Malcolm Dan tonight," he said. "He used to give me $5 and $10, but," he said, "tonight he gave me $16.25!"

He gave that money away. But he got it! It's up to him to do with it what he wishes. I never saw my father after that. Or anything.

So, anyone who comes to me with a story, after I question him and dig around, I can pretty well tell whether it's imagination or whether it's the real McCoy.

Willie Dunphy & His Brother

NOW, LOTS OF TIMES (*Bob Fitzgerald told us*), they say, you know, some people—if a person is in trouble—if they're away from home or somewheres in trouble, that there's a possibility of your seeing them.

Now, I remember poor Willie Dunphy—he's dead and gone—he was drowned at White Point. And he told me that he saw his brother.

He went to the barn in the morning before daylight and harnessed the horse. He was going after a load of hay. And he told me he fed the horse and put the harness on him. And he reached through and buckled the belly-girt. And when he straightened up, his brother was standing on the other side of the horse. And his brother was sailing, out of Lunenburg—Alexander.

And at the time that he said he saw him, they were on their way to the West Indies with a load of lumber. And the vessel waterlogged. And they were tied in the riggings—they had themselves tied in the riggings for three days and three nights. And at that time, that's where he was at—tied in the rigging of the vessel—before they were saved—before they were rescued.

Willie told me that himself—he's dead and in his grave. He told me when he straightened up, Alexander was on the other side of the horse. Definitely. And he said he didn't know what to make of it.

Why Joe David Burned the House
(English begins on page 43)

MOI, JE SUIS NÉ À PETIT-DE-GRAT EN 1911. Les vieilles du Petit-de-Grat contaient des histoires pour t'épeurer, elles disaient, "Si tu sors de soir p'is t'as pas dit ta prière tu vas voir le diable." Je l'ai vu une soirée though. Je restais encore dans cette maison là, je vous dirai à-propos d'ce maison là, le vieux voulait pas que je sortis le soir. Bien, j'y dit, "Je sors." Dans ce temps là je me baderais pas beaucoup, la religion me touchait pas. J'm'en allais p'is j'm'en venais quand je voulais. "Une soirée," y dit, "tu verras le diable. Je souhaite que tu voies le diable." Je pensais bien que je pouvais pas voir pire que moi.

Une soirée, ceci c'était quasiment dans le mois de décembre, un beau clair de lune, y avait tombé une petite neige, j'm'en venais. Y avait un pont là au bas de la grosse coline qui descend. Quand j'ai venu là y avait un gros maudit chien noir à travers du chemin. "Je peux pas passer, bien je passerai par la côte." Quand je descendis à la côte, il était là, allongé. J'monte back au chemin, j'monte p'is la même affaire. J'ai dit,

"Je passerai quand le jour se fera, sûrement tu vas t'en aller." Y était vers quatre heures du matin. Je restis là jusque temps que le jour se fit, p'is je rentre p'is j'me couche. Le vieux était chez nous. J'me levis le lendemain, tard vers huit, neuf heures. Y dit, "T'aie venu." "Oui," j'ai dit, "vous avez souhaité que je voie le diable, well, j'l'ai vu."

(Parlez moi de la maison.)

J'avais neuf ans quand j'on venu l'autre bout du havre là. Vous pouvez peut-être voir, la maison est pas là asteur. Voyez-vous la bâtisse qu'est là, la toute petite? Ça c'était notre morceau de terre. On restait plus haut que ça, d'icitte on voyait rien que la couverture.

Quand j'on venu là, moi j'avais rien que neuf ans, les autres enfants étaient plus petits. Je faisions pas de cas de rien et p'is une soirée ma mère rentrit dans sa chambre pour aller se coucher p'is tout d'un coup elle sortit de dedans sa chambre. Elle mandit à mon père ouère si qu'il avait sorti dehors. Y dit, "Non, j'ai pas sorti, pourquoi ça?" Elle était pas peureuse elle. Y dit, "Non, j'ai pas sorti dehors." "Ah! c'est bien," qu'elle dit. Ça s'est passé de même, elle a rien dit de plus.

Mais y avait une vieille qui restait là-bas, en haut du chemin. Ma mére allait la visiter pendant le jour. Elle a dit ça à cette vieille icitte. Elle y dit, "Hier soir, j'ai rentri dans ma chambre pour y mettre tcheuqu' chose." Le bébé était dans cette chambre, on était une grande famille. "Et," elle dit, "j'ai cru,"—mon père s'appellait Fred—"j'ai cru que Fred avait sorti dehors pour tcheuqu' chose mais il m'a dit qu'y avait pas sorti." Elle dit, "J'ai vu un homme passer dans le châssis." La vieille dit, "Une homme haut." Elle dit, "Oui, un homme pas mal haut." Elle le dépeindit, "Il avait un chapeau"— dans ce temps là ils portaient des chapeaux durs, manière comme des derbies—"p'is un half coat avec un ceinture tout le tour du corps." Bien la

38

vieille dit, "Sais-tu qui est-ce que c'est? C'est le vieux qu'appartenait la maison." Y était mort, eh! C'était un vieux qu'était mort y a longtemps.

Cette maison là avait été volée de lui. Si c'avait été volée ou quoi qu'avient fait, j'sais pas, mais c'avait été mal arrangé. La vieille a dit à ma mère, "Ça été mal arrangé." Y avient pas voulu payer le vieux et p'is nous autres on l'avait achetée, y nous avait rien dit, mon père l'avait achetée. Le vieux qui nous a vendu cette maison là il nous a dit qu'il l'avait donnée au diable. Un beau temps de venir nous le dire. S'il nous avait dit ca avant!

On a eu de la misère après qu'on a été là. La première soirée que j'avions couché là le lendemain je pouvions pas sortir. On pouvait pas ouvrir les portes, toutes étaient fermées, je pouvions pas sortir. J'essayons les portes mais aucun moyen de sortir. Y avait une école en haut, p'is c'est une petite fille qui s'appellait Berthina Arsenault—leur maison est encore là—c'est elle qu'est venue p'is qui nous a fait sortir. Elle passait pour les filles— pour aller à l'école—p'is elle rentrit. La porte était pas barrée mais nous autres on pouvait pas sortir. P'is ça la première soirée que j'avions couché là.

Après ça c'allait mal, le vieux se faisait mal p'is y pouvait pas travailler.

Après ça ma mère a mourit (accouchant dans cette maison), elle avait rien que quarante et un ans quand elle est morte. Moi, j'avais rien que seize. On a eu de la misère, là ça commencé comme y faut. Ça venait le midi et puis à minuit. T'attendais ça marcher en haut. Ça venait pour ouvrir la porte de l'escalier—c'était barrée dans ce temps là—ça allait pas plus loin. Mais on l'attendait pas s'en aller à sa place. Ça venait toujours à la porte de l'escalier. Là, ça passait pour un élan p'is le soir à minuit encore la même affaire. J'ai dit, "Ça icitte, ça va pas faire."

Moi, j'étais pas peureux. J'avais seize ans dans le temps, ils pouviont pas m'épeurer. Mais les autres, mes frères p'is mes soeurs, ça commençait p'is y aviont peur. Y aviont toujours peur. Dans ce temps là, c'était des scieaux d'eau p'is ils auraient pas été dans le tambour se chercher de quoi à boire à force qu'ils étaient peureux. Moi j'allais dans le tambour, je boivais p'is je quittais la chopine là. Je rentrais p'is je disais, "Maudit, c'est bon de l'eau."

Mais y aviont peur, y vouliont pu rester là. J'les avions mis sur la vieille Marceline Boudreau, ils restaient là. Ils s'en veniont à la maison le jour mais ils s'en alliont là le soir, ils voulaient pas rester. (*Votre père où est-ce qu'il était?*) Il travaillait à Mulgrave.

Ça fait je commençais à galloper un peu. J'allais à Petit-de-Grat y avait des belles filles là, j'allais galloper. Des fois j'm'en venais tard, mais une soirée j'm'en ai venu pas trop tard. Je m'avais pas rendu à Petit-de-Grat, j'avais trouvé des filles plus par icitte. J'm'en avais venu p'is j'avais été chez la vieille, il était passé minuit. Quand j'y fus la porte était barrée. Je voulais pas les reveiller ça fait que j'm'en va me coucher chez nous. Je rentre là—j'avais les clefs—je rentre là et je fis me coucher. Je pouvais pas dormir, j'ai dit, "Tu peux tropigner si tu veux mais j'm'en va pas."

Dans ce temps là t'avais pas des lumières comme asteur, c'était des lampes de kérosène. P'is le canister de kérosène était en haut dans le grenier. Moi, ma défunte mère elle—c'était pauvre dans ce temps là—tout le vieux butin quand c'était usé, elle coupait les morceaux dessus p'is elle gardait ça. Elle avait une grande boîte en haut qu'elle mettait tout ça dedans. Quand les autres butins s'adonnaient à dechirer elle allait chercher ça p'is elle racommodait.

Je va pour chercher le canister à kérosène et il me semble que je voyais de quoi sur la boîte qui

40

ressemblait des pieds. J'ai pensé à moi même, "C'est ti bien mais yeux qui fait ça ou bien si c'est vrai." J'partis pour descendre, là je déviris de bord, je fus aura de la boîte comme d'icitte au deep freeze, y avait une grande paire de pied blanc virée comme ça, le dessous des pieds viré par moi. Je me dis à moi même, "Je sais pas à qui les pieds, mais c'est des pieds." Je pris mon canister et je descendis mettre la kérosène dans la lampe. Je fus le porter en haut, c'était pu là. Mais je couchis dans la maison tout seul, tous les autres étaient partis. Tous les soirs ils s'en alliont. Je couchis dans la maison et p'is le lendemain je leurs dis.

Mais ça venu que je voulions pu rester là. Ça venait que c'était trop tannant, le midi p'is le soir, y avait tcheuqu' chose là.

Après ça y avait des pêcheurs sur l'autre bord du Cap-Auget. Quand on a eu abandonné la maison, le matin ils se leviont p'is ils voyaient de la boucanne sortir de dedans la cheminée, p'is pas de feu, j'étions pas là. Ou bien y avait une lumière sur le châssis p'is personne là. Y avait rien que moi qui bardaçait alentour moi et une de mes soeurs, mais elle aurait pas couché là.

P'is y avait un vieux, Johnny Goyetche, qui restait aura de nous autres, la maison est partie de de là. Y dit, "Ça gâterait ti quand même j'irais voir pour moi même." J'ai dit, "J'va quitter la porte débarrée." J'ai dit, "C'est pas utile que vous alliez avant minuit, vous attendrez rien avant minuit, ou bien le midi dans le jour." Y dit, "C'est bien, j'irai." Ça fait il y fut. Bien, je le watchais, j'étais alentour cette soirée là. Je watchais voir s'il allait y aller. Il y fut. Y restit à peu près une demie heure. Y sort de de là, y s'en va chez eux. Y dit, "Ce Joe là," je m'appelle Joe, "y est pas peureux, moi j'y restrais pas."

Le vieux voulait pas nous croire. Il disait que c'était pas vrai. "Vous dites que c'est pas vrai, moi je vous dis que c'est vrai. P'is vous allez coucher icitte." Ça fait il descendit de Mulgrave un samedi soir. Y croyait que c'était moi qui faisais ça—moi j'étais vicieux—je voulions pu rester là. "C'est pas moi qui leurs fait peur." Il s'en est venu coucher là et pour prouver que c'était pas moi qui faisait ça, j'ai couché avec lui. "C'est bien, je vais coucher avec vous. Pas asteur mais à minuit, quand minuit va taper vous attendrez." "Bien," y dit, "c'est toi qui rêve." "Vous croyez que je rêve mais j'rêve pas." Juste minuit, le voilà. Il dit, "C'est pas toi qui tape sur le rabri?" J'ai dit, "J'm'en va me lever d'icitte, vous verrez si c'est moi qui tape sur le rabri. C'est pas moi qui fait ça."

Tu sais lui il fumait la pipe, il allumit sa pipe, j'étions assis. La première affaire le voilà encore, la même affaire. J'ai dit, "C'est ti moi qui fait ça." Y dit, "Non, c'est pas toi all right, c'est vrai." "Bien," y dit, "tu dis que t'as couché icitte tout seul." "Oui," j'ai dit, "j'ai couché icitte tout seul." "Bien," y dit, "t'es brave." Ils ont jamais pu m'épeurer.

Mais en même temps y voulait pas sortir de dedans. Il voulait arranger la maison. Bien ma soeur p'is moi on a dit, "Il va pas l'arranger, c'est all right pour lui y travaille ailleur, nous autres sommes icitte. On peu pas dormir des nuits ou bien faut aller chez des étrangers, ça soute pas. On va maudire le feu dans ça icitte."

J'ai maudit de la kérosène autour de la chéminée, p'is j'ai maudit une allumette. On a brulé un bord de la couverture. Tu penses pas à tout. J'aurais pu me prendre mieux que ça, le mettre dans la nuit, tout le monde aurait été couchés p'is y avait pas de danger pour les autres, on était assez loin. On l'a fait all right. On a mit le feu, mais elle a pas tout brulé. Rien que le bord de la couverture. Le vieux l'a vendue pour $75.00 à Eugene Samson. Il est venu p'is il l'a défait p'is il l'a haulée au Petit-de-Grat. Il la quasiment toute perdue, toutes perdu les planches. Quelqu'un lui à volé ou bien ça disparu. Il l'avait pilé ou est-ce qu'il allait se bâtir mais quand il a venu là, plus que la moitié était partie.

Joe David, in English:

I WAS BORN IN PETIT-DE-GRAT IN 1911. The old women from Petit-de-Grat told stories to scare people. They would say, "If you go out tonight and you don't say your prayers, you're going to see the devil."

I saw him once though. I was still staying in that house—I'll tell you about the house (later)—the old man didn't want me to go out. "Well," I said, "I'm going out." In those days I didn't pay much attention; religion wasn't important to me. I went out and came home as I pleased. "One night," he said, "you'll see the devil. I hope you see the devil." I figured I couldn't see worse than myself.

One night, it was almost December, a nice moonlight, fresh fallen snow, I was on my way home. There was a bridge at the bottom of the hill. When I got there, there was a big black dog across the road. "I can't get by. Well, I'll go down by the shore." I went down the hill and there he was stretched out. So I went back to the road and there he was again. I said, "I'll get by when day breaks, surely you'll go away." It was about four in the morning, I couldn't go home. But I was able to pass when day came. I went in and went to bed; the old man was home. I got up that morning; it was late, around eight or nine. My father said, "You're back." "Yes," I said, "you hoped that I would see the devil. Well, I did."

(*Tell me about the house.*)

When I was nine years old, we came to the other side of the harbour there, maybe you can see where. The house isn't there any more. Do you see

43

the building that's there? The little one, that was
our property. We lived higher up; from here you
could only see the roof. When we came there I
was nine years old, the other children were small-
er. We weren't worried about anything. Then one
night my mother went to her room to go to bed
and suddenly she came out again. She asked my
father if he had gone outside. He said, "I didn't go
out, why?" She wasn't a fearful person. He said,
"No, I didn't go outside." "That's all right," she
said. It happened just like that, she didn't say
anything more.

But there was an old woman who lived up the
road. My mother would visit her during the day.
So she told the old woman, she said, "Last night I
went to my room to put something there." The
baby was in that room, we were a large family.
And so she said, "I thought"—my father's name
was Fred—"I thought that Fred had gone outside
for something but he told me he hadn't gone out."
She said, "I saw a man go by in the window." The
old woman said, "A tall man?" She said, "Pretty
tall." My mother described him. "He had a
hat"—in those days they wore hats, hard ones,
kind of like derbies—"and a half-coat with a belt
around the waist." "Well," the old woman said,
"do you know who it was? It was the man who
owned the house." He was dead, eh? He was an
old man who had been dead a long time. The
house there, it had been stolen from him. Actually, if they had stolen it or what I don't know. But
the deal wasn't done properly. The old woman
told my mother, "It wasn't done right." They
hadn't wanted to pay the old man, and then they
sold it to us—hadn't told us anything—my father
had bought it. And the old man who sold it to us
said he had given it to the devil. A good time to
tell us, huh? If only he had told us before.

We had problems after we got there. The first
night we slept there, the next morning we couldn't
get out. We couldn't open the doors. Everything

44

was closed. We couldn't get out. They seemed locked. We tried the doors, but there was no way we could get out. There was a school above, and it was a little girl called Berthina Arsenault—their house is still there—it was her who came and got us out. She was passing for the girls—to go to school—and she came right in. The door wasn't locked but we couldn't get out. And that was the first night we slept there.

After that things didn't go well. The old man would hurt himself and he couldn't work. After that my mother died (in childbirth, in that house); she was only forty-one when she died. I was only sixteen. We'd had trouble, but then it *really* started. It would come at noon and then at midnight. You could hear it walk upstairs. It would come to the door; at that time there was a door at the top of the stairs which was closed. It wouldn't go any further, but we wouldn't hear it go back. It always came to the door of the stairs. Then, it would stop awhile. At night, at midnight, the same thing would happen again. I said to myself, "This won't do." But I wasn't fearful. I was sixteen at the time and they couldn't scare me. But the other children, my brothers and sisters, it would start and they were scared. They were always fearful. In those days we had water buckets and they wouldn't even go in the porch to get something to drink. That's how fearful they were. I'd go in the porch, drink, leave the pitcher there and come back in and say, "Damn, that's good water!"

But they were scared, they didn't want to stay there. We had to send them to the old woman, Marceline Boudreau, they stayed with her. They would come to the house during the day but leave at night. They didn't want to stay. (*Where was your father then?*) He was working in Mulgrave.

Anyhow, I was starting to run around a bit. I went to Petit-de-Grat. There were pretty girls there. I went running around. Some nights I came

45

back very late, but one night it wasn't so late. I hadn't gone as far as Petit-de-Grat. I had found pretty girls closer than that. I had come back and gone to the old woman's house. It was past midnight. When I got to the house, the door was locked. I didn't want to wake them so I went to our own house. I went in—I had the keys—I went in and I went to bed. I couldn't sleep. I said, "You can roam around if you want but I'm not leaving."

In those days there weren't lights like now, we had kerosene lamps. And the kerosene canister was upstairs in the attic. My deceased mother—we were very poor then—would take the clothes when they were worn and cut pieces from them and keep them. She had a big box upstairs that she would keep them in. When the other clothes would get torn she would get these pieces and mend them. I went up to get the canister of kerosene and it seems to me that I could see something on the box that looked like feet. I thought, "Is it my eyes that are playing tricks on me or is it real?" I started to go back downstairs and I turned around quickly. I was near to the box as that deep freeze. There was a large pair of feet turned like this, the soles of the feet turned towards me. I said to myself, "I don't know whose feet they are, but they *are* feet." I took the canister and went downstairs to put the kerosene in the lamp. I went back upstairs, the feet were gone. But I slept in the house all alone, the others were gone. Every night they would leave. I slept in that house and then the next day I told them.

But it got so that even I didn't want to stay there. It was too bothersome, at noon and at night, something was there.

There were fishermen on the other side of Cape Auget. Once we had abandoned the house, they would get up in the morning and they would see smoke coming from the chimney, but there wasn't any fire—we weren't there. There was only me

46

who would hang around the house at all—me and my sister—but she wouldn't have slept there.

There was an old man, Johnny Goyetche, who lived near us. The house is gone now. He said, "Would it bother you if I went to see for myself?" I said, "I'll leave it unlocked." I said, "It's no use going before midnight, you won't hear anything before then. Or else at noon during the day." He said, "That's good, I'll go." So he went. Well, I was watching—I was around that evening—I was watching to see if he would go. He went. He stayed about a half an hour and he came out of there, he went home. He said, "That Joe"—my name is Joe—"he isn't fearful, I wouldn't stay there."

But my father wouldn't believe us, that this was happening. He said it wasn't true. "You say it isn't true, but I tell you it is true. And you are going to sleep there." So he came down from Mulgrave a Saturday night. He thought it was me doing it—that I was bad—but I didn't even want to stay there any more. "It isn't me that's scaring them." He came to sleep there and to prove it wasn't me doing it, I slept with him. "It's all right, I'll sleep with you. Not now but at midnight, when midnight strikes you'll hear." "Well," he said, "it's you who's dreaming." "You think I'm dreaming, but I'm not dreaming." At midnight, there it was. He said, "It's you knocking on the wall." I said, "I'm going to get up from here, you'll see if it's me knocking on the wall. It isn't me who's doing it."

You know he smoked a pipe, he lit his pipe, we were both sitting up. The first thing you know it starts up again. I said, "Is that me doing it?" He said, "No, it isn't you all right." And him, he wasn't fearful. "Well," he said, "you say you've slept here alone." "Yes," I said, "I've slept here alone." "Well," he said, "you're brave." They've never been able to scare me.

47

But at the same time, he didn't want to move from there. He wanted to fix the house up. Well, my sister and I said to each other, "He wants to fix it. It's all right for him, he's working away but we're here. We can't sleep at night, or we have to go to strangers, it's not right. Well, we'll set fire to it."

I put kerosene around the chimney and I threw a match. We burnt the whole side of the roof. You don't think of everything. I could have done it better if I had done it at night. Everyone around would have been sleeping. But we did all right. We set fire to the house but it wasn't completely destroyed, just one side of the roof. My father sold it to Eugene Samson. He sold it to him for $75.00. Samson came and tore it down and hauled it to Petit-de-Grat. He lost most of it, lost almost all the boards. Someone stole it or else it disappeared. He had piled it where he was going to build, but when he returned more than half the wood was gone.

John D.'s Father & the Re-Burial

I WAS BORN IN BAY ROAD VALLEY near
Bay St. Lawrence. My father's name was Duncan
H. MacDonald. His home was in Bay Road Valley. He was a farmer and he worked for the pro-
vincial government on road work, and he was also councillor for quite a number of years, Bay St.
Lawrence district.

I can remember when I was a young fellow
and people would tell those stories such as I'm
about to tell, and some very, very truthful people
would tell you some very convincing stories. And
I have no doubt in my mind that some of them
were true. I suppose there were a lot of them
pretty fictitious in many cases, but I have no
doubt but many of them were true.

My father was a young man at the time this
happened to him. It would be in the 1890s. He was
born in 1878, and he would be eighteen or twenty
when this happened. And he had been to church
Sunday evening. Church was at Aspy Bay, at the
little church—horse and wagon days then, of
course. And at that time there were people lived a
short distance in the direction of Cape North from
the church—Ramsey was their name. And one of
the girls there was Suze Ramsey. And my father,
after church he drove her to her home.

I don't know what time it was—it was night—
when he started back home toward Bay Road
Valley. And I don't know if you know it or not,
but at that time the first Transatlantic Cable had
landed at Cabot Landfall; and there were some
people working down there, living in the area—
people that were involved with the cable. And
there were also some local people living there.

So he was coming home, and he was passing up at what was then a MacDonald home right next to the road. There was a gate when you came in from the direction of Cabot Landfall, from the direction of the shore, before you come out on the main highway—there was a gate. So he was driving up the road, kind of a steep hill before you get to this gate—and he was just sitting back in the wagon, not taking too much notice of what was going on. The horse was walking along. And it was a very bright night. The moon was out, full moon. And he looked, coming from the direction of the shore, up through those houses where people lived, a road by those houses—there was a man coming out toward the main road.

Well, he thought nothing of that, because he thought it was one of the people that was living or working in there. But first thing he noticed, this fellow was alongside the wagon. And it struck him, the thought came to his mind, How did he open the gate or get over the fence so quickly? It didn't seem possible that he could do it.

So when he got up alongside the wagon, my father said to him, "Would you like a drive?" And at the same time he noticed that the man was wearing a uniform. He had an officer's cap on—it was a kind of Navy-type uniform. And he said what he really looked like was the picture of that sailor on the package of cigarettes. That's what he looked like. And he said he had high leather boots on.

When he asked him if he wanted the drive, he said, "No." But right then, there was a kind of a...my father knew there was something that wasn't just quite natural about this.

This fellow said to my father, "No, I don't want a drive, but I'd like you to do something for me." My father told him he would, if it was possible. So he told him that he was on this ship, a Scottish boat that had been shipwrecked on North Harbour beach. And that they had been drowned and their bodies came ashore on the beach. And he said, "My body is buried down"—at that time there was a cemetery at Cabot Landfall. All my people were buried there first. With the wearing away by the sea, erosion, their bodies were becoming exposed. So my people were moved up to the Aspy Bay cemetery. And this is what this fellow told my father—that his body was becoming exposed. And he asked my father if he would shift him in further. And he told him where he was from—Paisley, Scotland. And he told him his name was Anderson. And he told him where to get in touch with his people, his descendants. And my father told him he would sure look into it.

And then the fellow was gone. (*Disappeared or walked away?*) I don't know, really. I heard my father say, but I don't remember.

But he went home, continued on home. And when he went in the house his father, old John MacDonald, sitting at the end of the table, reading the Bible—and he went in and he told him what took place. But in the meantime, on the way home, he was wondering, Did I dream that or have a nightmare?—he was so certain that it was real. But anyway he told his father what happened. His father, who they called Red Jack, was a pretty hot-tempered fellow. And he just didn't take too kindly to what my father told him.

My father insisted that he have a look. Well, okay. They went over the next morning and went over to the bank, and there were the two leather boots sticking out of the bank. And they took the ground from over him. He was wrapped into a canvas, and his uniform was on him just like my father had seen him, only if you would touch it, it would disintegrate. And there was a piece of money in his pocket, you could see it through the uniform—I expect it was a half crown, from what I've seen of English money afterward.

51

They moved the body in. And he wrote to the address in Paisley, Scotland. Sent the money, and got back a letter and a plaid shawl.

They dug the body up and reburied him. (*Did they mark the grave?*) I don't think they did. I know I looked down there, and the only grave I can see there is a MacDonald fellow; he'd be a different MacDonald than I am. But there used to be—well, the major Protestant cemetery for that area was down at Cabot Landfall at that time. And I can remember myself going over there and looking and seeing a coffin sticking out of the bank. (*And your father would tell this story?*) Oh, yes. (*And over the years, he never doubted?*) No. (*And was that the only thing that ever happened to your father?*) Yes. That's the only thing supernatural I ever heard him mention.

Marie MacLellan & the Fairy Bow

MY FATHER, BIG RONALD, he was a great musician. (*How did he become a violin player?*) I can't understand it. We could never figure it out, why he was such a great violin player. Because he never had any special training. He just grew up, and he'd be in different places playing different violins. I don't believe he even owned a violin, when he was young. But he became one of the great violin players of his time.

He never did explain to us, he never told us why he was such a great violin player. But I always thought that it was a gift from God that he had. He didn't learn, in any specific way, except what he just picked up on his own. So it had to be a gift from God.

(*What did he do to make his living?*) Blacksmith by trade. He was in Inverness a long, long time. He blacksmithed. My father was noted for this: He'd take the most cross, kicky horse. And he'd just take him and he'd throw him. He had some knack—I remember him as a child—he'd take that cross horse and he'd just turn him over—like with one hand on his back. And he'd tie his feet, and he'd shoe him.

He used to work at this heavy, heavy work. Eight, nine, ten horses a day. And you'd say, well, his hands were so calloused and rough. And he'd take the violin and he'd play the most delicate, professional tune that you've ever listened to.

So it had to be a gift—I still say it was a gift. And many, many, many people, even in this day, would tell you that—what a delicate violin player, and yet what rough work.

I don't know where he got his violin, really, first going off. But as a boy, he had a homemade bow, as a kid. And he always told us the story at home about him being a little, little boy at home— he was eight or nine or ten years old, something like that. He was brought up in Broad Cove. He was brought up with his aunts. His mother had passed away when he was small. And he was brought up with his father's sisters. They had a big farm and a lot of cattle.

So the girls—a lot of older sisters—they were out taking the cows home one evening and—he always told us that, as kids—when his aunt gathered the cows and they were starting home, there was an arrow went by her, right on the hill in front of her. So she thought nothing of it; she thought, What a great switch to drive the cows. She just picked it up—there was a sort of handle on it. She drove the cows home. And she said, I'm taking this in the house—you know those old-fashioned homes in the country—and she just threw it in a basket and put it up in the back to dry, the stick, you know. She put it up on the sill—you know, the old-fashioned homes weren't sealed? And she put it up behind the wood stove, in a basket.

When my father started to learn violin, she took this little stick. And of course, she told him to go and get his own hair out of the horse. So he did. He made the bow, and he started to learn. And all his life, all our life—the fairies used to come for us. They always bothered us—they followed us, they braided our horses, they braided our cattle, they came to our places when we were growing up as kids, the fairies.

It was a sort of a fairy bow he got. The gift came through them. They gave him this little stick, and they were coming, I guess, and they bothered us all our life. You'd hang clothes on the line, and apron strings or anything—you'd go out

54

in the morning and the most gorgeous beautiful braids. There was no hairdresser could make them as pretty. The horses, they'd be all braided. They were around there all our life. And they say, wherever they are, you're always poor. And they sure followed us—they followed us all our life. Never left us alone. Whether they wanted that back, or what.

My father was working in a forge in Inverness, and he had this bow, you know, and he had it in a trunk with all his personal belongings. And it burnt in the fire. It went in the fire. So I was wishing we had had it, to put it in a museum. Wouldn't it be nice?

(*When the bow disappeared, when it burned, did the fairies disappear, too?*) Yes. They went, yeah. (*So you've never seen any evidence of them since then.*) No, not at home. Not at home, ever since it was burnt. But I can always, always remember—I used to say to Mom, "My goodness, can you understand?" I'd go to the barn and milk the cows or whatever. And I'd say, "How come everything's beautiful with braids?" And she'd say, "Oh, the fairies are back again." She knew. She used to see them. Little white men, yeah. Little white men, that's what they were.

(*Do you mean their flesh was white?*) Yes, and they had gray hair, and they were white. It's hard to describe. Just men, just little men. That's what she always said. "Oh," she said, "the fairies are back—they're after your father for that bow. They want it back." We didn't think anything of that. It's just like when we started to play for a dance at nine years old. We thought we had to do it. She always said that.

(*Did you or any of your brothers or sisters ever actually see the fairies?*) No, I don't think. Although sometimes you'd see little visions. Like you'd see shadows, like, around your clothes, and around different things. But you try to undo those braids! You just try to undo them. If you had a wash on the line—you know in the country they used to put strings of clothes out—if you had a wash on the line, everything was beautifully braided together, your clothes—it didn't matter what you had—were braided. Then you'd go to the barn, and the most gorgeous braids in the horses' manes and the horses' tails. You would really actually have to see it to believe it. I was sixteen, seventeen years old—I was old enough to remember the beautiful work they used to do. It was just unreal.

Ghost Stories from St. Joseph Elementary School

The Light in the Distance

by Jason Dennis

MY GRANDFATHER HAD BEEN WORKING IN A LUMBERCAMP in New Brunswick. He was on his way home and had gotten a ride to within three miles of his home. He had to walk the rest of the way. It was very dark and windy, there was no moon or stars and the road was a narrow, little-used country road.

My grandfather had gone about half way home when up in the distance he thought he saw a dim light shining through the trees. As he got closer the light would disappear, then appear, grow bright, then grow dim. Needless to say my grandfather was wondering what was making the light for he knew no one lived in this area and it was very late at night for anyone to be about.

As he rounded a bend in the road he saw the source of the light. It was coming from the tail-board of a wagon and by its dim light he could see a man trying to replace the wheel which had come off.

He walked up to the man who did not see him because his back was turned, and asked if he could help him. The man didn't answer. Grand-dad thought the man could not hear him because of the wind, so he touched the man on the shoulder.

Slowly the man's head turned and my grand-father recognized him as Mr. Jenkins, a person he had known for many years. But he looked very pale and his eyes were very sunken, so that they looked like two black holes.

Again my grandfather asked him if he could help and Mr. Jenkins just slowly nodded.

Together they replaced the wheel and without saying a word, Mr. Jenkins rode away. Needless to say my grandfather continued his walk home thinking not very good thoughts of Mr. Jenkins.

When Granddad got home, he went straight to bed without waking anyone. In the morning at breakfast, he told the family about meeting Mr. Jenkins, and as he told the story they stopped eating (and) stared at my grandfather.

Granddad said, "What's wrong?" and my grandmother said (that) two weeks ago on a dark, windy night at the same spot where he had helped Mr. Jenkins, a wheel had come off a wagon (and) a man had broken his neck and died. The man was Mr. Jenkins.

·

White Horse

by Cheryl MacQueen

ABOUT TWENTY YEARS AGO in Dutch Brook. My uncle was picking up his papers for his morning delivery, when he saw a carriage with two white horses pulling it away quite fast. Then he saw a man run after it. He knew something must be wrong for the horses to be scared like that. After they passed, he tried to cross the road but his horses wouldn't go, so he took the long way home.

The next day he heard that someone had been murdered where his horse would not go, so he told the police what he saw and they arrested the man, put him on trial and he was found guilty. He was also the last person to be hung by the county police.

A couple of months later my uncle went into the woods to gather wood and he saw the same man with a rope around his neck riding on the same white horse he saw the night the man was killed. And then the man disappeared over the river saying he would get revenge, and a year later from the murder my uncle became sick and died.

·

A Newfoundland Mystery

by Trent Sampson

ONE DARK, RAINY NIGHT in a fishing village in Newfoundland, a fisherman and his wife were preparing everything for his early morning fishing.

He would leave at night and return very early in the morning, while his family was sleeping. His wife would usually wake up long enough to yell out, "Is that you?" He would answer, "Yes"—and come to bed. His wife would get up and go downstairs to clean up the water off the floors and stairs, that came from his wet boots. And then she would return to bed.

One evening, they were going through the same thing, helping him get ready to leave. But this time he stopped and gave her a hug and kiss, which he normally didn't do till morning. His wife found it to be a strange thing for him to do.

That same night there was a terrible storm and his wife waited for his return. When the door finally opened and his wife yelled, "Is that you?"

59

and he answered, "Yes"—she was relieved to hear his voice. Then she went to clean up the mess which was bigger than usual.

But when she came upstairs to go to bed, her husband was gone.

She found out thirty minutes later that he was drowned more than seven hours ago.

So who was that man who came upstairs and wet the floors and stairs more than thirty minutes ago, and then disappeared?

•

Double Vision
by Jeff A. MacNeil

IT WAS A DARK, CLOUDY NIGHT in Piper's Cove. Mickie Kettie and Hector MacNeil were walking home. It was pitch black and hard to see. Mickie Kettie was a man who had "second sight." He'd see things before they actually happened.

Suddenly Mickie said to Hector, "Move off the road." "Why?" Hector said. "Because there is a funeral going by." "I don't see anything!" said Hector.

They moved off the road. Afterwards, Mickie said, "There was some strangers in that funeral procession I did not recognize."

Hector saw nothing and was quite scared by Mickie's vision. By and by, they came to Mickie's house. Mickie said, "Well, I'm home. See you later."

Hector still had to walk a half mile to get to his house. His home was a ways off the road and he had to cross a sluice. There was a log across the sluice by which one tiptoed carefully. Hector was so scared, he started running. When he came to the water and muck, he didn't bother with the log, but ran right through the sluice to the safety of his home. He was terrified.

A week later a man from Piper's Cove was killed in a mine accident in Glace Bay. The strangers in the funeral procession were some of his fellow workers from the Glace Bay mine.

•

The Vanishing Woman

by Jimmy Donnison

THE STORY I AM ABOUT TO TELL YOU IS TRUE. It happened to my great-great-grandfather who told it to my great-grandmother who told it to my grandmother who told it to me.

When my great-great-grandfather was a boy, about my age, he lived in England in a large old house in a lonely spot atop the cliffs of Dover. The house was surrounded by a big garden with lots of apple trees.

One day, when he was playing in the garden, a lady he had never seen before suddenly appeared beside him. She asked him to save two apples for her when they had ripened on the trees, and she would return for them later.

This he did, placing them on a shelf, but the lady never returned for them.

The apples remained on the shelf in case she returned for them. They did not dry up or rot. They turned to stone!!!

•

A Bad Christmas

by Jamie Dawson

IT WAS CHRISTMAS EVE and Peggy MacDonald was getting ready to go to Midnight Mass. Then suddenly she heard sleigh bells. She just ignored it but then she heard them again, so she went outside to see.

When she got outside she saw nothing, but heard a voice say, "Something bad is going to happen."

Twelve o'clock came and she went to church. Mass got out and she went home. She was asleep when she was awakened by sleigh bells.

She went downstairs and she heard a voice say, "Something bad is going to happen." This frightened her greatly.

The next day at twelve o'clock the phone rang and a voice said, "Something bad is going to happen."

Immediately after she hung up, the phone rang again. It was her uncle. He told her that her father died.

Believe it or not.

•

A Ghost Story

by Gary Addicott

THIS STORY TOOK PLACE IN FRENCH COVE near St. Peter's. We have a summer property there.

In the 18th century, an English ship came with

money for soldiers. The French were nearby, so they hid all of the gold somewhere near French Cove.

When they went out into the open water, they were attacked by Pirates. (The Pirates) looked for the gold, but there was none, so they just burned the boat. Later in time, they found some of the gold in between the walls of one of the houses.

They still don't know where the gold is. It could be sitting on our property.

Before we bought the property in 1977, Mr. Twist had owned the property for quite a long while. About a year before we bought it, a couple bought it and moved out in just nine months. We suspected they were looking for either the 18th century gold, or Mr. Twist's money, because he never had much money at all. So they suspected he hid it somewhere. But where!

In 1984, my parents and a whole bunch of my aunts and uncles were sitting around a big campfire. All of a sudden there in the background, about fifty feet from the campfire behind a kitchen tent burst into flames at the stroke of 11:00 p.m.

They thought the tent was on fire but it was just the hay behind the tent. The day after, my relatives were joking about how, "I wonder if Mr. Twist really has a fortune." And right at the stroke of 11:00 p.m.—the very same thing happened!!

Was it Mr. Twist telling us where the gold was? Was it Mrs. Twist who oddly disappeared, and was never seen again? Was it her telling us where she was buried? Was it a warning from the English sailors not to look for the gold?

To this day we do not know the answer....

A Big Pond Ghost Story

by Ryan Hollohan

THIS IS A STORY ABOUT SOMETHING
THAT HAPPENED to my Uncle Bruce. This inci-
dent happened many years ago in the small community of Big Pond.

My uncle's wife lived in a home in Big Pond
which was used for several years before they
bought it as a funeral home for the area. Every-
time there was a funeral, the custom was to nail a
cross onto the wall to keep away the evil spirits.
With this kind of history, you can see why the
house had a spooky feeling about it.

In the hallway upstairs there was a picture of a
very mean-looking lady. This lady was my uncle's
wife's grandmother. One night my uncle slept
over in the spare room. This spare room is where
the grandmother had died many years ago.

During the night my uncle was awakened by a
very strange presence. He was scared out of his
wits when he looked up and saw a ghostly vision of
what he swears to this day was the grandmother.
Everything seemed so real that he is still not sure if
it was the grandmother or just a bad dream.

•

The Suspicious Moving Chairs

by Shawn Murphy

WHEN MY GREAT-GRAND-PARENTS WERE
ALIVE, they lived in the country, miles away
from their neighbors. Because there were no
phones, people believed there were signs that told
you someone was about to die.

One of the signs was you would hear someone

sawing and hammering wood, as to build a coffin.

Another sign actually happened to my great-grandparents.

One night, everyone was in bed, when they heard noises downstairs. When they went to investigate, all the dining-room chairs had been moved around.

The next day, one of the neighbors came to the house and told them his wife had died during the night. He wanted to know if he could borrow the dining-room chairs for the wake.

Had the chairs been getting ready to leave the night before, or was someone or something checking to see if they were suitable to borrow?

It is still a mystery in the family.

•

The Forerunner

by Lynzee MacNeil

ABOUT SIXTY YEARS AGO in the time of wagons, there was a family—a mother, father, and two children, a boy and a girl. The father was a fisherman and he would go out to sea for weeks at a time.

The little girl, Sylvia, was scared to go in her room alone because she was scared of the dark.

One night, her cousin Issabel came to stay the night. Around midnight, Sylvia heard a noise.

She asked Issabel if she had heard anything. She said, "Yes." It sounded like a rumbling noise from a wagon.

They listened closely. Sylvia knew the sound of

all the wagons in the village. She didn't recognize the sound of this wagon.

The rumbling was coming closer and closer. It came to the house and circled it and went around again. Then it knocked on the door four times.

Sylvia woke up her mother and her brother Justin and told them the story.

The next morning, they told their neighbour, Mr. Campbell. He checked around the house but he didn't see any tracks. He said it must have been a forerunner.

The wife started to cry as she thought her husband (had) died out at sea, and she was waiting for a word on him. The mother was going crazy from worry.

Justin took sick and died.

As Sylvia and Issabel were waiting for the hearse, they heard a rumbling noise. As they stood in shock, it came closer and closer. It circled the house—this time they could see it. The man knocked on the door four times, took the boy and left.

●

Life After Death?

by Amy Boyko

THIS STORY IS ONE THAT INVOLVED my great-grandmother and her son.

In 1972, my great-grandmother was at home alone and all of a sudden she had a very weird feeling that something bad had happened or was going to happen.

She decided to have a cup of tea, and while she

was waiting for the water to boil, she heard a knock at the door. When she asked who was there, no one answered. She waited a while longer and there was another knock.

This time when she went to the door, there was a man there. It was her son, Art. She asked him when he had come to Sydney and why he hadn't told her that he was coming for a visit.

He did not answer any of her questions; nor did he enter her home. He told her that he had come to say he loved her and to tell her good bye.

He turned and walked away and waved to her at the end of the long hallway.

She was very puzzled by all of this and went to bed, but had little sleep.

The next morning her other son came and told her that he had very bad news for her. Before he could say anything, she said that she already knew what it was—her son Art was dead. Her other son was mystified and asked her how she knew, and she said that Art had come to say good bye to her the night before.

In fact they later found out that Art had come at the very same time that he was pronounced dead.

This is a true story.

•

The Piano Player

by Stacy Lynch

MY GREAT-GRANDMOTHER'S HOUSE was on the top of the hill on Victoria Road in the Pier. It was a small grey house that my grandmother and her sisters and brothers lived in.

During a heavy rainstorm in the autumn, everyone went to bed because there was really nothing else to do.

Just as everyone was going to sleep, my great-aunt thought she heard someone playing the piano but she was sure everyone was in bed.

So she got up out of her bed and went to her brother, John. John heard the piano too, but he didn't want to get out of bed.

Finally, they both went to the room where the piano was. They looked in the room and could see and hear the piano, but they never did see the piano player.

That same piano is now in my grandmother's living-room and some night when everyone is asleep, the piano player could come back.

•

William's Return

by Janie Astephen

THIS IS A STORY I KNOW IS TRUE because my grandmother told me. It is a story that happened to her grandmother, Katherine.

One day many years ago when Katherine was a little girl of eleven, a strange thing happened. The war was over and they were waiting for Katherine's older brother William to come home. Her mother had prepared a big feast and all her relatives and neighbours were there.

Katherine decided to walk down to the gate so she would be the first to greet him.

When he finally arrived, she was so happy she cried. He told her of all his experiences and how at night when the owl hooted he could only think of them at home. He gave her his gold watch and said, "Now I will always watch over you."

He told her to run ahead and tell the others he would soon be with them.

When she got to the house everyone was crying. William's friend Ben, who had been in the army, had told them William had been killed the week before. He had all (William's) belongings to return to the family. He said the only thing they couldn't find was William's gold watch.

That night Katherine cried herself to sleep by the hooting of the owl.

·

The Uninvited Guest

by Stephen Gillis

MR. HUGH MACDONALD was a well-respected blacksmith in Sydney. He was a quiet single man living in the home of his deceased grandfather, Hugh.

One day as Hugh was walking home from work he saw a mysterous woman staring at him. He glanced at her and kept on walking but she called to him and said, "Hugh, come here." He walked over and said, "Yes?" The lady then told him she (was) from his past, here to avenge her death. She then disappeared as quickly as she appeared, leaving Hugh trembling with an eerie feeling.

Entering his home, in deep thought, he noticed a lamp burning in the pantry. Seeing this, he reached for his rifle, loading it slowly moving toward the light. The winds around the house wailed as the floors creaked and shutters slammed. He approached the corner of the pantry, and there before his eyes stood the mysterious woman with piercing eyes and her uplifted arm revealed a sharp dagger ready to strike.

Hugh froze in his boots shouting, "Who are you and what do you want from me?"

She replied in a moaning voice, "I want you, Hugh MacDonald, the man who caused my death many years ago."

"I am not." He said, "Hugh, the man you are seeking, is dead."

When the word "death" was spoken she lashed out, cutting Hugh's forearm. Losing his balance, he crashed into the chairs causing the gun to fire. The bullet struck the oil lamp knocking it to the floor and setting the rug on fire. The flames caught her dress and with a harsh cry she disappeared.

Hugh, stomping on the rug, realized he couldn't control the fire. As he dashed to safety on the front lawn, he turned back for one last look and saw the mysterious lady in the upstairs window screaming in pain.

Many say she still haunts Hugh MacDonald's grave above the house on the hillside.

THESE GHOST STORIES won First Prize in the *Cape Breton's Magazine* Local History Contest, 1990.

John R. & Bessie MacLeod: Stories of Their Old Home

NO, NO, IT WASN'T THIS HOUSE. (*This is Bessie speaking.*) It was just down below here. That house is taken apart. But I'm telling you, really, it was spooky. And then we moved out. I was never scared when I was there. I heard lots and lots and lots of things there. And after we left—we only moved up just across the road—I went down the next day for dishes that I left at the house and, it was so funny, when I got to the door—if there was a dish there covered with diamonds, I couldn't go in for it. I froze right at the door. And I just couldn't—and I was looking at the dish in the pantry, through the window—just at the door I could see it. No, sir. I was so scared I couldn't go in that house.

And when I was in there I wasn't a bit frightened or anything. I'd stay alone there in the night. But when I left there, everything came, boy. That's the time I was scared. But I wasn't scared when I was living in it. I could go as far as the door and I would just freeze right there. I could not go inside.

(*But things were happening when you were living there?*) Yes. But while I was there I was okay. It didn't seem to bother me. I used to hear walking. And if you'd be in the kitchen, in the dining room, you'd hear somebody coming downstairs. And you'd be in one room and you'd hear whatever it was walking into the other room. When you'd be in bed upstairs through the night you'd hear the walking down below, pulling dishes and opening the doors. That's what happened that night we heard that man coming in. John R., tell it. You tell it better. Tell him about the night the man came in.

John R.: I'll have to tell that the last of it. We had just moved in. Thirty years ago. (*Did you ever hear stories about this house?*) The old people, yes, the old people did. *Bessie:* I think that's why they moved out of there, the family that owned it before. They never told till after they sold it that that's why. *John R.:* They used to see a woman coming down there. *Bessie:* Yeah. *John R.:* She'd go in the house. They couldn't see her. They'd see her going in, that's all.

My aunt was over there one night playing cards. She'd be 150 years old if she were living. And Mr. MacDonald had a black horse. In the barn. There was an old kitchen there—Dr. Chisholm was born in it—the late Dr. Chisholm of Margaree Harbour, born in that kitchen. She was over then, and she looked out the window—an awful storm on—and she saw this black horse looking in the window—great big beautiful-looking horse—and she told Mr. MacDonald, "There's a black horse looking in the window." "Oh, hell of it," he said, "the little black horse must have got out." And he took the lantern and went out and went over the barn and he came in and he said, "Oh, I put the horse in."

But the horse wasn't out—but Mr. MacDonald put it that way so the women wouldn't get scared. They were seeing, hearing things before I went there.

(*Take me back. John R., was there nobody living in the house when you moved in?*) My uncle Joe MacKinnon bought that place. He came home from out north. He bought that farm, from Mac-Donald. I used to be over there with him. I wasn't married then. We were shingling and painting the barn. My uncle this day went to town—went on a little toot—he came back, he drove down to the

72

place and he put the horse in the barn. He went over to the house, he opened the door. Sometime in the night—I don't know when he came home—but whatever met him at the door, he didn't go in. He went out to the barn and he took the robe out of the wagon; and there was hay on the threshing floor—and I caught him there in the morning and I asked him what happened. "How is it you're sleeping here and a big, beautiful house over there?" "Look, John R.," he says, "I'll never, never sleep in it. Or go in it." And neither did he.

Bessie: And they were awful good people. *John R.:* The people who owned it were very, very good people—whatever was wrong there.

Well, anyway, I moved from a place they call Egypt. Upper Margaree. Southwest Margaree, Egypt. Moved down. And I wrote to my uncle and he gave me the house. And we moved in there. This noise was going on. When we'd go to bed we'd hear everything moving and going and a table move and dishes moving and....

Anyhow this night my Aunt Teresa made the card playing. Bessie says, "John R., we're going to the card playing." A snowstorm on. I didn't want to go. I was working in the mines and I didn't want to go. She coaxed me so we went. The storm was so bad, we got as far as my father's. My father and mother were in, living alone. Went in. And my father said, "God, John R., you getting crazy, out on a night like tonight." I said, "Aunt Teresa got a card playing and I'm going to go." "T' hell," he says, "with the card playing—you'll get lost."

So my mother made tea and we were in talking. Went back over to the house. Walked back. Oh, we couldn't hardly see a hand ahead of us. We got down there. Went in and her mother was up and she had fires on and we had tea and went to bed. Her mother went upstairs ahead of us.

73

And she told me, "John R., lock the door."
"Maw," I says, "I'll lock it. The bodachan won't
get in tonight." *Bessie:* That's the little old man.

John R.: My uncle had a Yale lock on the door.
There was a storm door and there was a big hook,
heavy hook on it. I put the hook on the storm
door. I shut the door and I put the Yale lock on it.

Well, this dog, this German police dog was
down in the kitchen. We just got upstairs and I
put my foot across like that—I was opening the
laces. Well, holy jumping God. We thought the
side of the house came in. And this went through
the house, same as you took a 1700-pound horse
and went right down through the hall, right down
into this old kitchen. My mother-in-law said to
me, "John R., there's somebody in." "I'll tell the
world there's somebody in. I'll go down."

Her grandfather's tool chest was over in the attic; little wooden mauls in it they used to have
long ago to drive pins. I went over and got this
maul, boy. She followed me down with the lantern. Looked at the door. Same as I left it. Same
as I left it. There was a little place underneath the
stairs there. Opened that. I went underneath that
and I searched it. Searched every inch of the
house—well, the old kitchen you couldn't get in
there; I had it all boarded up. We searched every
bit of down below—nothing. Went upstairs back.

I just set on the bed, boy. *Bessie:* The little dog.
John R.: Oh, the dog. Yes. The dog came upstairs.
And he was so scared he went to get in the bed
and he hit his head in the bed and he jumped
back and he drove and he went underneath the
clothes. And he stayed there. Well, we went upstairs. And Mr. Man went through. And he took
the same thing going out with him. *Bessie:* Yeah.
Came through the dining room, down the hall. He
was just like a horse that would have iron shoes
on him. And the house shook, just shook. The bed

74

shook. I was sitting on the bed and the bed shook when he went through the two doors. Went right back the way it came. That's a true story.

John R.: Anyway, one night, this MacNeil came over. Aw, they all knew we were hearing things in the house. And MacNeil came over and this night we were talking.

And this man came in the door. I guess he was six-foot-four if he was one inch. And he filled the door. He just filled the door there, coming into the dining room. And he was there and he was staring right at me. He had this long slicker on right down to his ankles. And he had his slicker all closed up. And he had two straps and two brass big buckles for those straps to go into to keep it shut. And he had a cap on him—I'd say it was a captain's hat—with a great big badge in the front of it. And he stood there for about 20-25 minutes in the door and I was watching him. And MacNeil jumped from his chair and he went over behind the stove. And I was watching the man, see would he move. And whatever happened, I took my eyes off the door. I went to look at something and I looked back and there was no man.

So MacNeil wouldn't go home alone. And the lantern was on the table there and he went and he lit the lantern and I told him I wasn't going over there. It was as bright as day outside. "You're coming," he said. And MacNeil's a man not scared of nothing. So, I had to go with him. Walked along the road—the lantern between us— to his place. I put him in the kitchen. I left the lantern there and I walked home. Somebody would have thought I was crazy with a lantern, the night as bright as day. Went to bed. And that was it.

Bessie: That was it for *that* night.

(Were you scared going back that night?) John R.: I wasn't a bit scared. I'm not scared of noth-

ing. (*You didn't really think this man would hurt you.*) I was hearing it so much, so often, you see. I was hearing the walking and the going in the house....

That barn was about as far as this trailer from the house. I came home from Margaree with a load of hay. I go in the threshing floor—open the threshing floor doors and I drove in—took the horses out of the wagon and I put them in the stable. Fed them and went in the house. Bessie said, "John R., I didn't milk the cow." "Well, I told you, Bessie, to milk those cows before dark. Not to be going near that barn after dark." So there was no milk for one of the children—one of the babies. So we had to go. And the lantern was up in Upper Margaree. I left it up there. And we went out, took a handful of matches. And got our way and got the cow and I milked the cow. Told her, "I feel funny. There's something wrong here." And she never said a word. Left the cow and went out and I shut the barn door.

And there was a hollow right near the barn, close to the door. And it was always full of water. And here, I had my head down and I was walking. And I looked and I said, "Bessie, look where you're putting your foot." There she was, she was going to put her foot right on a man's throat. And she looked and she started squealing and hollering. I went straddle legs on the man. And I told her, "Go in the house. I'll hold him here. Go in." She wouldn't go. She started screeching and hollering. And pulling me. I said, "Go, go in. I'll find out who he is." He had a khaki pants on, a pair of brown shoes and a jacket. Nope, she wouldn't go in. So I had to go in with her. And my mother-in-law came out with me. And when we went out there was nothing.

Bessie: And it was so funny. When we went out it was so dark that you couldn't see your hand ahead of you. And when we came out of the barn,

76

everything was so bright that you could see him so plain. And I can see him there yet. And I was just picking up my foot—I can see him yet lying down in the water. (*Was he under the water?*) No, he had his hand under his head. And it was his head, mostly, that was in the water. A big puddle of water. I didn't know him. (*Was he the same man you saw in the doorway?*) *John R.:* I wouldn't say yes and I wouldn't say no. *Bessie:* What was so funny, how bright it was. I said when we were coming out of the barn, "Gee, didn't it get bright!"

John R.: When I left the place, John Simon MacDonald took it—and I told him to be careful, not to go near the barn after dark. He said, "I know everything that you were hearing." John Simon was from Cape North. Wasn't scared of nothing. Didn't care what it was or where the hell or what. "All right," I says, "you'll see for yourself but," I said, "keep out of the barn." But he was hearing things in the house himself—John Simon was hearing things and he was telling us.

John Simon was fishing—and this night it was raining and pouring and his wife wouldn't go for the cow. I would not blame her a bit, raining and pouring. John Simon came home and no cow and he had nine or ten—he had ten kids. And they were only small. Well, he had to go and get the cow. He got the cow. Put her in the barn.

And he went back home to the house. When he came back, boy, this animal was in the drain. It came from behind the cows and the horses. His two eyes, John Simon said, his two eyes was a fire as big as buckets and fire coming out of his nostrils and out of his mouth. The wagon was across the horse stable door, little ways from it. This animal was coming out and John Simon start backing out—and the stretcher of the wagon caught him right in the knees, and turn a somersault on him. He said that beast went right through the wagon; he said it went right down into the brook.

The next morning I was going over and John Simon was out. He had a bottle and he was slashing at the barn with this. I saw him in a couple of days. I said, "What were you doing when I was going over the other morning there? You had a bottle." "Aw," he says, "you had the truth, John R. The devil came out of there. You'll never catch me again in the barn." *Bessie:* He was splashing holy water. *John R.:* Yeah. He thought he was going to put the devil away, but I don't think he did. And in two days time John Simon packed up and moved and went up to Cape Mabou.

(*Do you have any idea what it might all mean?*) No, I do not. (*Do you feel any of it was trying to do you harm?*) No, not a bit. Didn't hurt me, didn't do nothing.... Fred MacIsaac, himself and Joe MacRae were up there. They're both dead. When we'd go to bed, we'd take the lamp with us upstairs. And when we'd put the lamp out, they'd watch. When we'd blow the lamp out they'd know, well, they're in bed. Down the kitchen and front room and dining room would all light up. What was doing it I don't know. They didn't know.

(*What finally happened to that house?*)

Bessie: It was torn down. *John R.:* I tore it to pieces. I found a glass jar, down in the silling. Full of ashes. I took it up here. And they went out of their minds. They said, "Throw that in the brook. Get out, get with it, get, get. That's somebody that died. And he was burnt." I said, "You're crazy." I went and I threw it in the brook and the bottle went to pieces and the ashes went down the brook. I hauled a piece of the house up here. I had it below there, had it for a barn. Tore it apart. All went. Nothing ever happened. The old barn fell down. Nothing ever happened.

Bessie: Whatever it was, it was somebody that was...troubled.

Noel Morris's Encounter with the Devil

in Micmac & in English

KI'S SA'Q, AKNUTK NUEL, TELI
AMALWI'TA'TITL JIPI'N, TA'N TELI
WTAIWASNA MNTUA NE'KI PEJI
MITTUKWALJEK. KE'SK TO'Q TELI WLI
NPAJ WIKUAQ, JIJUAQA NUTUATL
NA'TUENL I' MTEWO'TMLIJ
EPTAQNJI'JUO'KUOM, AQQ NKUTEY
KESIKAWETESKAWEJEL. APP NA TO'Q
WISQIW JENTESK. NA KWETNU'KWALSIT
KISI APAJI NPAN, ETLITE'TK PASIK
TLKUSIN. KE'SK SUEL KISI NPAJ APP
TA'PUEWEY KI'STO'Q APP NUTUATL I'
MTEWE'LITL NA'TUENL. NA TUJIW TO'Q
MENJA'SIT AQQ ELIET A'SE'K NAJI
ANKAMATL ME' WENL KISI PISKWA'LIN
WI'KK. NA TELI PISKIPUKUA'SIT WLA
A'SEY NA NEMIATL MNTU'L KAQMILITL.
LPA TO'Q MU TALI KWTAYAKUKL.
SKMTUK PIPANIMATL TA'N KOQOEY
MENUEKELIJ. MNTU TO'Q KELUSA'SIT
TELIMATL "MENUEKEY JI'NM, AQQ KISI
WISUOQTESKMULANN
AMALKEWAQNIKTUK, NA EIMA'LUL
KI'L!" NITAPTUT ANKITA'SIT TO'Q
KISIKUO'P JIPI'N. TA'N TUJIW KISITE'TK
TLI WISUOQTESKMUATAL NA TELIMATL
"A." WTUTESKATITESNU TI! E'PLEWI
WSIKEWIKWA'SIT TI TO'Q WLA MNTU.
ANSMA KETLEWITE'TK
WISUOQTESKMUAN KISIKUO'PAL AQQ
KETLEWITE'TK MU ALU'TUKLIN.

MEKWAIKE'L TO'Q WLA A'SEY

KAQMA'SIT AQQ POQTHTESINK MNTU.
JIKEIWATL TO'Q MENAQA KISIKUO'P
ANKAMATL TA'N TELTESINLIJ.
OQOTEYJI'J E'PLEW TESINK TO'Q WLA
MNTU. KAQISI MILIKTESINK AQQ KAQISI
MILIKTESKL WKWATL. PA'QLAYATL
KISIKU TA'N TELI E'PLEWTESINLIJ, KATU
ME' KI'KAJIW MU TALI KWTAYAKUKL.
KAQMIT TO'Q PASHK ESKMALATL
KAQTESINLIN KWLAMAN APP NEKM KISI
AMALKATEW WJI WISUOQTESKMUATAL.
KLAPIS KATU TO'Q KAQTESINK MNTU.
NIKMA'TJI'J SIWIET TO'Q AQQ
TEKNAMUKSIT. TELUET TO'Q "MU
NAQMASIANUK AMALKAMK
TE'SIPOWIKATAMK." KAQMA'SIT TO'Q
KISIKU APP NEKM MEKWAYIK.
KWETNU'KWAISIT KISI
WISUOQTESKMUAN WLA MNTU'I.
NITAPJI'J E'PLEWTESINK TO'Q APP NEKM.
MIAMUJ WISUOQTESKMUATL MHTA
LMA'LUKUTAL. WESKEWIKWETUTK TO'Q
MNTU. ME' KI'KAJIW ETLITE'TK
WISUOQTESKMUAN KISIKU'L, NA TO'Q
KE'SK ANSMA PEM KAQTESINK KISIKU
AQQ MNTU ANSMA KISITA'SIT LMA'LAN
JIJUAQA TO'Q KISIKU POQJI
KLUTJIEWEYTESTOQL WKWATL.
OQOTEYJI'J JIPAQATESINK TO'Q MNTU
AMSKWESEWEY NEMIAJ TELTESINLIJ.
OTI MELKI JIKEIWATL TO'Q MNTU. KI'S
APP TO'Q KISIKU KLUTJIEWEYTESTOQL
WKWATL AQQ MNTU ME' APP AT
JIPAQATESINK. NA TO'Q SI'STEWEY
TELTESTULIJ WKWATL NA TO'Q MU
KAQMUTMUK MNTU AWSAM
WE'KWATA'SIT. AUNASI
KIWA'SKHPUKU'TESINK, PANTA'LATL
KA'QNN AQQ POQTHTUKWI'K
WESIMUKWAT. NA NEMIAJ TO'Q KISIKU
WESIMUKWALIJ NA POQTHTESKUATL
KESIKAWA'SIT TO'Q MNTU AQQ ELT
KISIKU MU KNEKK ELKUAQL.

80

ELTESKUATL TO'Q MI'SOQO
ASOQMKAQNKE'L TA'N SUEL ETLI
WSASKMALIJ AQQ SIAW WIJE'WATL
WE'KAYIW NEMIAJ PASIK PEM
PUKTEWSILITA AQQ SIAWI KSIKA'SILITA.
MU NAJI LUKWAQNA'LUKUKWA NA
NUKU' APP MI'SOQO PEKIJE'KEK.

Noel Morris, in English:

A LONG TIME AGO, Noel (nicknamed Jipi'n) told the story about how he frightened the devil once when he was visited by him. Evidently while he was sleeping soundly in his house, he suddenly heard someone tampering with his cupboards, and making loud noises with his feet.

Then, just as suddenly, everything quieted down. Since all was quiet again, he attempted to go back to sleep, thinking that it probably was just a dream. Just as he was dozing off the second time, again he heard someone noisy. This time he got up and walked to the other room to see if anyone had walked into his house.

As he entered the kitchen, there stood the devil. He wasn't the least bit frightened of him. He simply asked him what it was he wanted. The devil spoke up and said, "I want to take a man back with me and if I can beat you in a dance I'll take you!" The old man stood back and thought of this challenge carefully and as soon as he thought of a way to beat him in a dance, he said to the devil, "Okay, I accept the challenge!" The devil smiled broadly upon hearing the acceptance. He was certain he could dance better than the old man and that he would not go home empty-handed.

The devil proceeded to the middle of the room and began his dance. The old man watched him very carefully, watching his every step. The devil put everything into his dance. His whole body twisted in every way and his feet showed many different steps. The old man was surprised at his one-hundred-percent effort, but still he wasn't afraid. He just stood there and waited for him to complete his dance so that he could begin his own dance and attempt to out-dance him. Finally the devil completed his dance. I guess he was mightily tired and had put on awful sweat. He turned to the old man and said, "It's not easy to dance when you're horsefooted."

So the old man took his turn and stood at the middle of the room. It was his chance to beat him. He displayed one hell of a dance himself, knowing that he had no choice but to win. Otherwise, he goes for a trip with the devil.

The devil had a broad smile on again. He was still convinced he had the old man beat. But just as the old man was at the last stage of his dance, and the devil thinking he's got him, (Noel) positioned his feet in such a way as to make a sign of the cross. The devil was apparently shaken upon witnessing this move for the first time. He watched the old man carefully as he continued his dance. Again the old man crossed his feet to form a cross which shuddered the devil even more. Upon making his move the third time, the devil was devastated and couldn't take anymore. He turned quietly, opened the door and ran. When the old man saw this, he took off after him. The devil was moving at a good speed but the old man was not to be left too far behind. He chased him as far as the old bridge where the devil almost slipped, and stayed with him till he saw him turn into a ball of fire and then disappear. He was never bothered by him again till long after.

Malcolm Campbell with Donald John MacMullin

HOW ABOUT THINGS THAT YOU HAVE
HEARD THAT NEVER COME TO PASS? Do
you remember, Donald John, the year—there
was a lot of snow. And there was crust on it, you
know—some of it would hold you in the fields—
remember the shiny crust used to come on the
snow? Well, one evening my Uncle Alex and his
brother-in-law, Donald John Pine, they came up
to our house just in the evening. It was dark almost; they had a lantern. They were out at the
door, taking the snow off. And you remember
John R. Campbell. He had a horse bell—oh, it
was a dandy—you'd recognize it above everybody else's in the neighbourhood. And we could
hear the bell, and you could hear the horse
breaking up the crust, and the sleigh.

Now I don't know if my grandmother heard it
or not. There was my grandmother and my mother and my Uncle Peter and Uncle Alex and Donald
John Ferguson. And we were listening to this.
Now the road wasn't broke up on what we call the
back road at all. They were coming through the
field—up by the barn—and they were going out
at the other end. Anyway, they thought, Well now
that's John R.'s bell and he's coming home from
Sydney and he's drunk and he's asleep and the
mare is following straight up and she's going to go
the logging road—lovely road—oh, the double
sleds and the chains, it would make a road just
like the floor here—everybody followed that—it
went right through the neighbourhood.

Donald John and Uncle Peter took the lantern
and they went out to head them off—and there

wasn't a sign of anything—not a living creature—
there was no horse, no track.

Now that horse bell: Angus MacLean had it on
one of his cows and she lost it. And John R. is
dead and all of these people except myself are
dead. And that never came to pass and it never
will. How can it? But we heard it, all of us.

Donald John MacMullin: I'd sooner say that
it's coming true than not. Maybe somebody got
that bell.

Malcolm: God only knows. There is no other
sound in the world that would be the same as a
horse and a sleigh breaking through the crust—
because he takes a step and you don't hear anything until he gets the next one—there's this in-
terval in-between. Because your traces are fastened to the shafts itself and your sled moves—
there's no whippletree....

Donald John: Well, I was up to Neil Hughie's.
There was a commotion in the air I think anyhow.
And Neil asked me, "What's the meaning of seeing a white light with a man, around a man?" I
said, "Well, now, Neil, I don't know. I never saw
that. But I always heard that the white light is not
bad. But if it was a really red light and seeing
where you shouldn't, it's supposed to be tragic, a
bad light."

But Neil got sick now. And nobody paid very
much attention to him. He wasn't well and we
started (work on) the bridge out there. But Mary
told me when I came home—"I'm going to see
how Neil is." And it was cloudy, getting rainy and
so forth. And when she got back she said, "Mike
wants you to go out tonight, he figures his father
is worse." And it started to rain. So I put on my
sheepskin coat. And Mama was always, "Where
are you going?" "Well, Neil is not well." "Well,
have you got the holy water? Have you got in

84

your pocket the holy candle?" I had more than the fellow would believe.

This side of the house I took the coat off, give it a good shake. Put it on again and went in. Someone came to me: "Daddy's taken a turn." And I got the holy candle and put the light to it and walked down the hall, and I could see that Neil had the pallor of death. You're on your last. So I took his hand and just turned him over, and he was dead.

Well, that's what he saw himself. He saw the white light, the candle light that I had down to see him, around him, come out of my coat pocket.

But how is it that so many at that time could see it, and not too many see it now? Unless religion is getting too strong or something. That it's kind of blurring you to it. We have more preachers and more churches and it seems to me that they're dampening those things out. Could be that.

Malcolm: There's too many other things going on. They could see them and they don't notice them. I never saw anything except lights myself but I heard noises and stuff in connection with the dead.

But I often wondered, now, when Mary Hayes died. The hearse started out the road here and then stuck. And I came out there and put the coffin on my wagon. And nobody ever heard tell of anybody seeing that (before it happened). You'd see an odd one but there would be hundreds of things happening no one would see anything about. You would have seen a forerunner about that because it would have made a lot of stir—the hearse come out from Sydney and they got stuck in the bog there. The fellow that was driving had to walk out to Hayes to tell them about it. I had an express wagon and went out a bunch of us with lanterns, and this was of course the empty casket they were taking out to the house. And the next day I took the remains in to the Meadows schoolhouse and they met us with the hearse. But nobody ever saw a thing.

The only thing I could connect with that—a week before she died Mary Hayes was over at our house. She walked, of course. The road was bad. It was in the spring and it was muddy. And I said I'd drive her home and I drove her to the gate. I was gonna help her out of the wagon and I just caught her and put her down—and honest to God she wasn't any heavier than that bottle of beer. I was surprised. It bothered me afterward. She was a small woman but she had a big coat on her and she wore her clothes down to her ankles in the old-fashioned way—but I couldn't get over it, how light she was. But then the following week she was dead.

Donald John: Of course you know, on the Mira River, I don't know who was drowned. They had to come in and got the gear for digging. There were lights around the water. And there were lights seen coming to the barn. That light was getting the gear ready. I was walking and the light turned. The light came down to the end of the lake and it turned and it made a little noise, made a noise when it switched at the end of the lake and I was about 30 feet from the road. I heard the swish.

Malcolm: I was walking out from Sydney one evening in the fall of the year. I got a drive out to the end of Woodbine Road and I started walking. I was coming up just to what they call The Barren there between our place and Ferguson—and this light shined on the road like cars at that time. Peter MacKinnon, he had an old Model T Ford—and gosh I thought that was him and I stepped to the side of the road. And I could hear this little rumble, like a motor. If I stayed there yet, there was nothing pass me. So I just kept on walking home.

But John Archie Campbell and Hughie Ferguson were coming out from Sydney with a horse and wagon and they picked up Ned Brown's daughter and they were coming down at the foot of Dutch Brook Hill—she got awful scared—they didn't know what was wrong with her—they couldn't see anything—but there was this ball of light, about the height of the shaft, following right along. Now, that was all right.

Maggie Ferguson was looking out the window toward the road. There was an opening where they could see a bit of the road. And she saw this light going by. Johnny Hayes and one of the boys, just turning at the end of the Woodbine Road with a horse and wagon—they saw it. And it went out back of Lower Woodbine Road and it went up the way of John R. Campbell's. The MacLean kids were in their fields and they saw it. And it went in back of John R. Campbell's. And there was never a god-damned thing.... The only thing I know: the power line came down through there.

Donald John: It wouldn't have any connection with Roddy Cameron?

Malcolm: No. Roddy didn't go there. He went from Collins to Sydney, the body, and from there to the cemetery.

Donald John: You know, you might hear things that would frighten you—various things—there *were* things...but I don't know. There was something like that saving me. It was right here alongside of me. I was out to Victoria Bridge. And we went to a dance, myself and Hughie. And the lake and swamps were alongside the road, you know. I was never at the place before. It wasn't so far from my aunt's but I was never there. And somehow or another Hughie went ahead, and I missed him. I could hear them on the ice, and I could hear them: "Don't go out that far, that's bad."

Well, I was standing alone. But I heard walking ahead of me. And I heard ice breaking and I went after him and I couldn't catch him. And that walking came to my aunt's clearing. I didn't catch nobody, didn't see nobody. But the walking was there, I could hear the walking, I could hear the clamper of ice breaking. He kept me on the road.

But I don't believe those things you hear near the graveyard at all.

Malcolm: Nor do I—the fellow's so scared he hears anything.

Donald John: You're scared, you know, and you're gonna hear that—but I don't believe it. I don't believe a man is going to die there's nobody going to take his footsteps.

Nothing ever hurt my grandfather physically, that he ever met, he told me. No. He was 96 when he died. And he could thread the needle—black spool thread—and he could sew a patch on this knee. He could see signs, you know, that there was something going to happen. It's just a matter of a kind of film on your eye. You'll see it plain enough. And if you see it, it's true. If you want the double sight you can have it. Yes. My grandfather. Anything at all that was moving, he'd see it.

I was taking him home, in a sleigh. Coming down Salmon River he says, "Donald John," he says, "do you want the double sight?" I don't know what he was thinking of. I says, "No, Grandpaw. My sight is good." So it was then. Good yet, thank God. But it was damn good then. He said, "I've got the connivers." (If) I put my left foot over his right foot and I'd put my right hand over his left shoulder—"and you're going to see what I see. You'll look at it." I said, "I don't want to see what you're looking at. Go ahead. Have a good look at it, Grandpaw. I don't want no sight. No, no, no. I got plenty sight." "Oh, well," he said, "that's good enough. But I'll give you the double sight."

88

Well, I shaved people and I dressed them and watched them and put them in the casket—there were all kinds of them dying out back—but I never saw anything interfering with myself...at no time.

A Twice-Told Tale

I HAVE AN IDEA THAT IT WAS A REAL TRUE STORY (*Mary Ann MacDougall told us in Ingonish*) because my mother and my father were together. She was a servant girl working at this house. He used to go to see her. Anyway, her mother was always against her going with my father. You understand? But she was dead now. So they kept on going together anyway.

This night, where she was working, the man had gone away. He had no children. His wife had died and he had hired my mother for to work there. And my father, he was of a mind of always wanting to sing or something like that—so he was sitting onto a chair—and the chair was back to the wall. And it came near nine o'clock. She wanted him to sing this song, so he started to sing this song. He said the song was only about half over when he heard this bang on the wall. He thought it was just some young fellows were frightening him. So he—he didn't open the door then. He just hollered and he said, "Try it again." So he sat back in the same position in his chair again.

He kept on with the song. The next time, he said it hit that hard that you thought for sure that the house shook. So anyway, he jumped, put his chair back—and he went to the door, went to open the door—and when he went to turn the knob one way, the knob twisted the other way. He tried it two or three times. He went and sat down, and he began to get weak. He asked my mother for a drink of water. And she found that he couldn't speak.

I'm going to bring it out right—doesn't matter if you're a Catholic or a Protestant, doesn't make any difference—but she ran to a holy water bottle, and she got the holy water and she put a little stuff into his mouth. And his tongue, she said, was right thick then, couldn't get a word out. But after a little while, he began to come back to himself.

He got up again. He went to go open the door. He opened the door this time easy.

There was a woman standing side on him. And there was a piece tied under her chin to the top of her head, and they knew who it was, too.

So that's the time they went out of their mind altogether with fright. They both nearly died that night. And when the man of the house came home—that's the man she stayed with—he wanted to find out what was wrong. So they up and told him. So my father said, "I can't go home. I wouldn't go outside that door tonight." The man said, "Stay where you are." So he had to stay there all night.

He knew who she was anyway—it was her mother. My mother's mother. He said he knew her as soon as he saw her. (*And she was the one who didn't want them together?*) Yes. That was almost her last words to my mother. She wanted her to part with him. But she never listened to her.

So then he saw her a second time. (*Where?*) John James remembers the second time. I'd have to find that out. But the second time he saw her, he had to go to the priest, told the priest about her. Priest asked him, did he think he knew her.

Said, "Yes." He said, "You won't be bothered any more." So he had a Mass for that woman. And from that day till he died, he never saw her, he was never frightened any more.

So that seemed kind of true. Because I know I could believe my mother, same as I could believe God Almighty, anything she told me. She'd never forget that night, she said, as long as she ever lived.

The Second Telling:

WELL, MY SON, I'LL TELL YOU (*John James Whitty, Mary Ann's brother, told us in North Sydney*), like the other fellow said, I never saw too many things—but there are other people that saw things down there. I'm telling you right here, and I know it to be the truth because my father saw things. He told me one night that he and my mother—they were going together then—they called into a house close by the church (in Ingonish). The reason they called in is because my mother's cousin was in there—she was keeping house for a poor fellow who had lost his wife, died about a month before that—and they were going to stay all night there.

The man of the house wasn't home, went over to his sister's, he wouldn't be long.

So Papa went to the house and went in. And my mother was there, she had all her clothes—she was going down to Green Cove, she was going to cook down there for a bunch of fishermen. And Papa was going down with her, Papa was going to fish down there. Anyhow, they went in.

Dark came. They were no time there when dark came. The girl keeping the house said to Papa—she knew he was a good singer—she said, "Sing us a song." So Papa told me he started to sing the song. He told me he put his head back like this to

sing the song—first thing, boy, something struck
the house, outside. So he said he stopped singing.
A little while after that, he said, it came in the
porch. And there was a big door, and the door was
locked. And a button—an old-fashioned button
they used to put on the old homes. There'd be no
way you could burst the door and get in the porch.
And when my mother came in, whether it was a
suitcase or whatever she had, she never brought it
right in the house. She left it right out on the
porch. And he figured it was the bear. Figured the
bear burst the porch door in.

He said, "Boy, it was making this racket on the
porch." He called out, "Look out there, I'm going
to shoot you." He said it never moved, whatever it
was. Well, boy, he told me, "Me son," and I'm not
telling you a lie, boy, he said, "I went to the door
and I opened the door—I *went* to open it. I turned
the knob, and when I turned this way," he said—
and he was a strong boy—"when I turned this
way, it turned the other way right against me."
He said, "I knew right then, boy, it was something
that wasn't very nice. I knew by the feel."

"Well," he said, "that's okay, boy. We went
away back and sat in the sitting room, the three of
us. The noise stopped, the racket stopped. So by
and by," he said, "we went back out again to the
door." The girl had the lamp. He said, "I went to
the door, I caught the knob, I turned the knob.
She had the lamp and your mother was behind
her. And," he said, "I pulled the door open—I
opened the door. And when I pulled the door open
this woman was there—and she was standing," he
said, "side out." And he said she had the white
piece like they used to put on you when you died,
to keep your mouth closed. Said, when he opened
the door, this woman was standing, side on.

He said, "I never took time to see who it was,
but I shut the door." He went into the room and
he said he felt for sure that they could see his

92

mouth, because he figured it went in an awful shape—his mouth. He said his tongue got that big, he didn't want them to see it, from the fright he got. He ran and grabbed the bottle that was there, full of holy water. He took a drink.

Anyway, he stayed like that for a long while, with his head buried down, so they wouldn't see his mouth. He said there was nothing wrong with his mouth afterward, drank holy water—"Boy," he said, "there never was money enough that we'd ever go to that door again."

But whatever that was, it struck that house— and I'm telling you—my mother told me too, and that's one thing with her, she'd never tell a lie— said it hit the house that hard that it pretty near knocked every dish that was in the house down. Whatever it was. That's as true as God Almighty. And she said it went. There was no more.

But anyway, when the fellow of the house came home, he rapped at the door and they wouldn't let him in. Made him come around to the other door. And he came in, and they told him.

He said to the girl, "Listen, did you give all her clothes away?"—his wife, who had died—she had died in that house there, about a month before that. "Yes," she said, "I gave everything away, clear of one dress." "Well," he said, "you get that away tomorrow." And Papa and he sat up that night, never closed their eyes. And the next day, Papa and my mother went down to Green Cove.

And there was a big dance that night (at Green Cove). An awful lot of families, lot of homes down there, what they called summer homes—till the fall, when they'd move to their other homes. They went to the dance. And he had a dance and he said he was warm, and he and a Donovan fel- low—they went out to get cooled off. And Papa told me, "Boy," he said, "I filled my pipe, and I lit a match. I was just putting the match to my pipe—it was a nice beautiful night—when I felt this thing, blew right in my ear, like wind. This hot wind." At the same time, this fellow said to Papa, "Tim, look at the woman!" And he fainted stone dead, the other fellow that had seen her. And Papa said, "The curse of the Lord on your soul"—and he made one drive at her. But he never saw anything.

They got the other fellow up, put water on him. Said he went out with a lantern—and the only two tracks that were there were his and this fellow that fainted—although this fellow saw this woman. And he got frightened, the curse he had put on her, because he said it must have been someone who was dead. Had to be. There is nothing that could get in that porch, unless it was a spirit. The door never was opened. And then down there at Green Cove the next night.

So the next day he walked up from Green Cove. He had a dollar. It was only a dollar then for a Mass. He came up and saw Father Duncan. And he was feeling real scared, he said, Father Duncan was an awful cross priest. Father Duncan said, "Tim, I hear you got a fright." He told him the whole story, about the next night and the curse he said—this was the only thing, when he had to tell the priest about the curse that he put on her soul.

"Well," he said, "have you got a dollar?" "Yeah, I got a dollar." "Well, I'll take this money and I'll have a Mass for the repose of the soul, whoever that person is. You needn't worry. You'll never be troubled again."

And never again, he never saw that woman after that.

Bill Daye:
Stories about Deer

A DEER OUT AT FRAMBOISE that I caught. I was walking down an old path through the woods, and I noticed a deer's face, a doe—his horns and his head were hidden quite a bit, but I could see his chest. I got a good sight on him and I fired at him. I thought he dropped.

When I went up there—it was about 25 yards away—when I got up there, there was the inside of a deer, the stomach and all the intestines, laying on the path. The deer wasn't there.

So I figured somebody had just shot a deer there. But I didn't hear any shot before. So I began examining around, and I see a little dampness and broken grass and fur. So I began following it. I see where he had slid over a big log that was about up waist-high laying sideways, and there was damp, water like on it. So I followed his trail here and there till I came to the river. And here was the deer laying in the river, washed and cleaned and killed with one bullet.

What had happened—when the bullet struck his chest, it stopped spinning around. And the jacket had a ragged edge that slid down between his stomach and the inside of his hide and cut right out through the fur, the entire length of the deer. And when he jumped with the shot, his stomach and everything fell out. So, that's a strange story.

•

I USED TO WEAR MOCCASINS, oil-tanned moccasins, going through the woods hunting deer, so I wouldn't make a sound, when you'd crack a stick and walk—you'd be just as quiet as a deer. So this night I was coming across the barren, and it was pitch dark, black dark. I had to feel the path amongst the blueberry bushes with my feet to know I was on the path. It's hard where people had been walking so much. And I keep walking on this little hard spot, and going along.

I was smoking cigarettes at the time. So I thought—there was a big rock I knew was along the path—and I said, "Now, I'm going to have a smoke." So I took out a match and a cigarette, and I scratched the match on that rock, and when I put the match up to light it—a big buck blew it out right in my face.

He was coming right towards me. If I hadn't stopped to light the cigarette, I would have run right square into him. My feet were as quiet as his, me with the moccasins on. Well, boy, I stood and I shivered—a cold chill went up my back like I was frozen. I couldn't move. And he flew by.

And there was a big barren on one side. And he got out in that barren, and was snorting and whistling. I was so mad, I up with the rifle and I fired in his direction. I swore at him, and I said, "You scared the life out of me—I'm glad that you didn't kill me!"

So, I forgot all about him. But it was a terrible scare I got. If I hadn't lit the cigarette, I would have walked straight into him—our noses were together.

So the next year I was out around, I found his bones out in the barren, where the shot that I fired had killed him.

Dan Angus Beaton Tells about the Headless Woman

(English begins on page 99)

BHA RAGHNALL MAC AILEIN OIG 'na sheol-adair, comhla ris gach uile rud eile rinn e. Agus bha e 'na dhuine òg agus b'fhìor thoigh leis a dhol gu dannsaichean. Ach turus dhe na turasan a bh'ann, thainig e gu baile beag agus bha dannsa ann agus bha e 'son dhol a dh'ionnsaidh an dann-sa. Cha robh ann ach soithichean sèolaidh aig an am ud, agus ghabhadh e trì neo ceithir a lathai-chean dhaibh mu'm faigheadh iad am badhar a bh'aca a chur dheth agus badhar úr a chur air.

Bha an dannsa bha seo, bha aca ri dhol cross beinn 'ga ionnsaidh—mu cheithir mìle cross a' bheinn agus mu dha mhìle deug mu chuairt air a' bheinn. Fhuair e mach far an robh 'n dannsa, ach bha seann duine fuireach an sin: "Chan eile math dhuitsa," ars esan, "a dhol cross a' bheinn an deidh dol fodha na gréine. Bi a' ghrian fodha mus faigh thu cross, agus duine sam bith a chaidh ann an deidh dol fodha na gréine, cha chualas mu dheidhinn tuilleadh. Thig spiorad 'Colainn gun Cheann' as an uamha agus beiridh i ort agus thig do mharbhadh. Tha coiseachd uamhasach agad ri dheanamh a' dol mu chuairt. 'S fhearr dhuit fuireach aig an tigh."

"Biodh sin mar a bhitheas," thuirt esan, "tha mise dol a dh'ionnsaidh na dannsa agus tha mi dol cross an rathad goirid." Thuirt am bodach ris, "Tha mise dol a dh'fhàgail beannachd agad, chan eil dùil 'am gum faic mi thu gu bràth tuil-leadh." "Biodh sin mar a bhitheas," thuirt Ragh-nall Mac Ailein Oig, agus dh'fhalbh e.

Cha robh e fada sam bith gus an deach a' ghrian fodha, agus a' "Cholainn gun Cheann" a bha seo—bha e feitheamh rithe. Agus bha e air innse, nan cuireadh duine gu bràth sìos i air a druim, nach biodh i na bu laidire na cuileag an uair sin—nach biodh spionnadh sam bith innte.

Bha Raghnall air a cheum. Nuair a bha e tighinn goirid dhan uamha—cinnteach gu leoir—chunnaic e "Colainn gun Cheann" a' tighinn amach. Colaidh uamhais de bhoirionnach mór uamhasach gun cheann idir oirre. Bha eagal air, ach thuirt e ris fhein, "Feumaidh mi an gnothach a dheanamh neo bi mi reidh." Dar a bha e dìreach mu coinneamh, rug iad air a chéile, o swing gu swing, chuir i air a ghlùinean e dha no trì thrupan 's bha ise air a glùinean aice trì no ceithir a thrupan. Mhair an t-sabaid mu uair neo còrr: bha coltas mu dheireadh gun robh i 'm brath an gnothach a dheanamh. Leis an eagal a ghabh e, theannsa gun d'thug e dha barrachd spionnaidh. An dòlas mur tug e aon draghadh uamhasach oirre 's chuir e air a druim i. Dar a fhuair e air a druim i, cha robh i na bu laidire na gin eile.

Bha i aige an uairsin agus thuirt i ris, "Leig as mi nis 's cha chuir mi trioblaid air duine tuilleadh." "Chan eil sin dol a dheanamh a' ghnothaich idir," thuirt esan, "tha mise dol 'gad thoirt a dh'ionnsaidh an dannsa."

Chuir e air a ghualainn i agus dh'fhalbh e leithe. Chaidh e cross a' bheinn leithe 's ruig e 'n tigh dannsa, null 'san oidhche. Bha i ag ochanaich 'sa gearain gun a toirt ann, ach thug e ann i co dhiubh.

Dar a ruig e, thainig a h-uile duine bh'anns an tigh amach a choimhead a' chulaidh uamhais a bh'aige. Cha b'urrainn dhaibh a thuigsinn no cha mhór a chreidsinn gun gabhadh leithid a bhith, gun a shealltainn dhaibh gun robh i aige. "Nis," ars esan, "tha mi dol gad' thoirt astigh dhan tigh gus am faic iad thu anns an t-solus—an rud uamhasach a bha deanamh a' chron a bha thu deanamh 'san uine bh'ann." Thuirt ise ris, "Ni mise rud sam bith a dh'iarras tus air an t-saoghal—sin an rud mu dheireadh air an t-saoghal a dh'iarras mi—na toir astigh mise dhan tigh."

"Mata," thuirt esan, "ni mise sin. Theid thu sìos," ars esan, "anns an t-suamp (swamp) uamhasach tha seo far nach cuir thu trioblaid air duine fads' a bhios saoghal na shaoghal, 's fuiridh tu ann gu bràth. Cha teid thu air ais anns an uamh nas mò agus leis an sin far am faic a h-uile duine thu, faodaidh tu falbh air do shocair."

Agus dh'fhalbh i, dha no trì throighean bho'n talamh, agus bha i gabhail ochanaich de dh'òran goirt bog, dar a bha i falbh. Tha sin na phort pìobaire aca dh'ionnsaidh an lathair diugh. Mar a bha i gabhail an òrain:

'S fhada bhuam fhein tha bonn Beinn Eadalainn
'S fhada bhuam fhein tha Bealach a Bhòcain
'S fhada bhuam fhein tha bonn Beinn Eadalainn
'S fhada gun teagamh tha Bealach a Bhòcain.

Agus cha deach a cluinntinn gu bràth tuilleadh agus sin agaibh naidheachd air "Colainn gun Cheann."

Dan Angus, in English:

OH, THAT'S A LONG STORY. That was Raghnall Mac Ailein Oig again, you know. He was travelling, sailing too—he did different things, you know. And he came into this town. And this Headless Woman, she caused an awful lot of trouble in Scotland. She lived in this cave.

To cross the mountain was about three or four miles, but (to go) around the place was about ten or twelve miles. And if you'd go across the mountain, all day, back and forth—there was a trail right across this cave—never bothered. But as soon as the sun'd go down, you're finished. If you crossed after sundown, you'd never be seen. She'd come out and grab you.

But there was a fellow in Scotland, and he was a great piper, one of the best pipers that ever lived. And he was sent—he was given this chance to go into the cave. They could pipe so perfectly in Scotland, that they could just tell what was in the cave, you know. And if he'd go in, and tell, and if he could come out—he'd have his freedom. But it was up to him. He had his choice. The gallows. Or to go into the cave, and pipe, and tell them what he was seeing. He could go in there and pipe, and tell them on the pipes, you know—that's the only way they could hear. It gave the message outside, of everything that he was seeing. Understand? If he could get out of the cave after telling them, he'd be free.

So he decided that he'd prefer the cave. So he went into the cave with the pipes, and he started his piping. This great piper. And he started describing. He told them all of everything (he was) seeing, so many skulls of those men that were killed, and all this thing. And then he described this Headless Woman coming towards him. And he said—I'll say it in Gaelic—"Truagh an Rìgh nach robh orm 's trì làmhan: da làmh anns a' phìob agus làmh anns a' chlaidheamh. Pity God that I didn't have three hands: two hands in the pipes and one in the sword." You know—one using the sword. When this Headless Woman was coming at him. And he was piping, telling everything.

100

And then they heard the pipes quit, and they could hear him swinging the sword—Hnaa—Hnaa—until at last everything quit. And that was the last they ever heard of him. He, too, died in the cave. And all this was going on for many years.

But anyway. This Raghnall Mac Ailein Oig—years later, he came to this certain town. And there was a dance. And he was a young man and he wanted to go to the dance. But he'd have to go twelve or fourteen miles around. But there was only around three or four miles across the mountain. But the man told him when he asked him, "How many miles is it to the dance?"—he said, "There's no way you could go across the mountain. The sun is just about setting. And you'll never get by the cave before sunset. So you'll have to go around the mountain, and it's a long way. Nobody ever crossed." "Well," he said, "I'm going to take my chance." He was a good strong man, a powerful man. So he started across. "Well," the man told him, "we'll never hear of you again."

So he started across the mountain. And sure enough, as he was coming close to the cave—he knew that there was such a person—he had heard of her, you know. But he wasn't scared of anything, this Raghnall Mac Ailein Oig. And when he saw this Headless Woman coming at him, he was prepared for her. She made for him and she grabbed him. And they got into a fight. But legend had it that if you could ever get her down and get her on her back, she'd lose all her strength. So the fight took hold, from swing to swing. And she had him on his knees a couple of times. And if he did he had *her* on her knees. Until at last he landed her right on the broad of her back. And when he did, she was no stronger than anyone else that felt strong. There was nothing to her any more.

So. "Okay," he said, "now I have you." So he said, "I'm taking you to the dance *with* me, so the people can see you." She pleaded and begged for him not to take her to the dance house. "Oh, yes," he said, "you're coming to the dance house." So. "Oh," she pleaded, "don't take me there." And he said, "I don't care how much you plead, you're coming."

So he threw her on his shoulder. As the other fellow said, "I'd sooner anything else on my shoulder." But he took her anyway. And he kept on across the mountain, and he had her.

And he landed her at the dance hall. And he had her. And when they saw what he had, when the people saw what he had, they about went crazy. It was dark. And in those days it was candles—you understand me? "Now," he said, "we're taking you into the house, so *everybody* can see you."

"I'll do anything in this world, and promise anything in this world, but don't take me in the house. Anything in this world you ask, but don't take me in the house." And everybody was around listening.

"Well," he said, "in that case then, okay. I'll let you go. But you have to go to the foot of this mountain into this awful marsh, at the foot of this mountain, where you'll stay in this meadow forever, where you'll bother no one as long as there'll be life. And so you can go. But you'll bother no one no more."

And she left, walking about three feet above the ground. And he said, "You'll return to the cave no more." And when she was going, the tune—they play it till today—was:

'S fhada bhuam fhein tha bonn Beinn Eadalainn
'S fhada bhuam fhein tha Bealach a Bhòcain
'S fhada bhuam fhein tha bonn Beinn Eadalainn
'S fhada gun teagamh tha Bealach a Bhòcain.

And she left, lamenting and mourning that she never could return to her cave no more. She never was seen or heard after. And that's how he stopped her. That's that story for you now.

Charlie MacDonald: When the Taxi Became a Hearse

HE CALLED ME UP ABOUT NINE O'CLOCK IN THE NIGHT, at the hotel. He said, "Charlie, will you help me out tonight?" I said to myself, "Tonight!" I said, "Yes." He said, "Come up about ten o'clock and pick me up."

So I went down and picked him up. Here he came out: a pick and a shovel and an axe and a crowbar. "Lord God," I said. He came over and he put it in the back of the limousine. And we started. (*You didn't know what it was about.*) No. I said, "I guess we'll get there. A lot of timber coming in. The roads are pretty good." You know, the wide timber sleighs. It was in January.

So, my God, made good time going out. There was moonlight, and chains on, you know. He said, "We'll stop here." So we went in there. And the old fellow was up at the big Waterloo stove, making tea. "Oh," he said, "you fellows are just in time. I've got a pot of tea." So, pot of tea. And I scrumbled around in their pantry and I got a piece of homemade bread and molasses—I couldn't find the butter, so I took molasses. I didn't know how long I was going to be.

So he said, "Where does So-and-so live?" Went

103

to the window and looked. "See that house away up there? Well," he said, "that's his house up there." Moon shining on it, you know. No tracks up or nothing.

So Lord God, we went and we started. And I said to him, "Is the man living? Has he got to go into the hospital?" "No," he said, "he's dead a week. He's all frozen," he said. "Oh," I said. "We should have taken a sleigh." "I'll make a sleigh," he said.

My God, we had a job to get up on the crust. You'd probably make two steps on the crust and then you'd go down a foot, and up. Finally we got up there—the shovels and pick and everything. He had to pick away the door to get it open, you see. The snow was frozen against it. Well, that's why he knew, he did that before, you know. Well, I had an idea, too. 'Cause I was brought up in the country, I knew.

So we went in. And a little stairway—the front door, we clawed it open. And he smashed a—it wasn't locked, but there was a handle like that— he had to hit that with the axe. (*A latch.*) Yeah—in order to get the door to push open. So, this is about two o'clock in the morning. So anyhow, we went in. Oh yeah, we had a lantern. That's right, too, he had a lantern. We lit the lantern before we went up.

So, we went up to his—upstairs, now. There was just a plank stairway—no railing, no nothing. And the steps were about that far apart. Eight inches, yeah. There were about seven or eight of them. So, we got over.

There he was—frozen in the bed. Hands up; knees up—like that. (*Charlie has his hands and knees raised up. He has his mouth open.*) And mouth open. Lord God. I said, "We're going to have a job to get him downstairs." He said, "He'll go down." We took him over to this—he rolled him kind of sideways to get him out through a couple of doors. And he got him to the top of the stairs and he gave him a push. And he tumbled down the stairs till he hit the front door that we came in on.

(*You rolled him down.*) He rolled him down there. (*Rather than carry him.*) Oh, didn't carry him, no.

So, got him outside, the moon was shining. He said, "You can shut the lantern off. Save the oil, we might need it." So, here's what he did: he tied rope around here. Ankles, 'cause they were sticking up. And his hands. And lashed it up around his neck. And down. Put it around his shoulders. (*His own shoulders.*) Yeah. Took him down, like if he was pulling a sleigh behind him, to the highway where the cab was. And got him down, got him in the car.

And (that same) old fellow came out (of the other house), and he asked us if we wanted another cup of tea. He said, "You'll have to come in. I need the cups." So we went in and had another cup of tea. And, started for town....

So, that was fine.

.

The following winter—this, I still feel bad when I think of it. The next winter, it was in March. All right. (A fellow) called me. He said, "Charlie, there's a man here with a coffin. And," he said, "I got the loan of a truck—a small truck." He said, "He can't drive. And I can't go. But he'll pay you if you'll take the coffin and him in the truck. His father is dead out there a couple weeks, and he wants to try and fix him up."

So, I knew the old man (that had died).

So anyhow, we went with the truck, and talked, going out. He was so glad that I was going to do it, you know. Came out, and he said, "Now, Charlie," he said, "getting handy there." We had good four-foot sleigh track all the way out—good—and the truck had chains on. It would go right along, you know. Didn't take us long to get out there. Anyhow, he said, "I guess we can't get into the house, Charlie."

So we got out and we carried the coffin. We had a lantern—he had a lantern, and he had an axe, you see. So, I got out. I got started getting the coffin down. He said, "I'll go over to the door, make a track, Charlie. We'll carry it over. I guess," he said, "we'll have to put it in through the window because we couldn't get the coffin around the porch door and in the kitchen door."

Now I heard him hitting the window and breaking the glass, you know. I was waiting for him to come over and help me carry the coffin. Finally he came over. "Oh," he said, "I got the window open good, Charlie. And I left the lantern inside." 'Cause we had moonlight outside. So we got over to the window. "I'll go in," he said, "and you push the coffin in to me." Got in. He had the lantern lit. I got in afterwards, got in after the coffin.

So we went over to his bedroom, where the old fellow died. Here he was, just like the (other) fellow—feet up, and arms up. "Well, well, well," he said. "What do you think of the neighbours, Charlie—there weren't anybody here when he died—and left him stretched out. Now look at the mess," he said. "We can't get him in the coffin."

And, so he went out around the kitchen with the lantern. He came back in with a saw—a bucksaw! (*Oh, no!*) Yeah. I said to myself, "What in the hell is he going to do with that?" "Now," he said, "Charlie, you hold this leg." And he sawed it off there. (*No!*) All right—it was still bent. He put it on the chair—and I didn't have to hold it—and he sawed it there. That made two chunks. He did the same with this one. And he sawed the arms off here. And he had the body from here up.

He laid that in, and put a suitcoat on him. Because the coffin came up—it only opened.... (*The top half, yes.*) And he put the rest in down at the foot—packed it in there. And took—he found nails—and nailed the second—this part—open, and this part—wood—to get him in there. But when he closed it down, he nailed that so they couldn't open it. Left him there.

(*So he put the whole man into the coffin, nailed it shut.*) And nailed it shut. And it wouldn't be touched until they got the grave dug and took him to the graveyard with the priest, and buried him.

Margaret Brown Tells of Things Seen

THIS GOES BACK TO WHEN I WAS A YOUNG GIRL, working at the fish plant in Dingwall. And nothing else has come out of it.

I was working in the fish plant, and our house was just up from it. You could look right up and see the house. The hour was about three in the afternoon. This woman came around the corner. She was not a woman of this world—dressed like this world today. She was all dressed in black and her clothes came down to there, and she even wore black gloves. She came around the building. The door was closed. She put her hand up like that and she went right in. We didn't know anything about it. We all saw her. We thought it was somebody came up the back way. I had a sister, and thought that's who it was. But the long clothes....

So we came home and we were inquiring, and Mother said, "No, there was nobody came in." The next day around the same time, the woman came again. She just put her hand up like that and she went in. Two girls from the factory went right up, and went right in the house. My mother was in the pantry baking biscuits; my sister-in-law was asleep with the baby on the couch. "Who came in?" "No one." And they went right through the house. Nothing.

Some people around there started to get scared. There were quite a few—about 40—working in the fish plant. The next day, they all sat there on the side of the road, and there was an old lady among them—she was at that time about eighty years old, and she had never seen a thing in her life—and she said, "If there's anything going into that house, I want to see it." She was one of them that went up, and she sat on the bank.

Fair three o'clock this woman came. She put her hand up like that—and this is the funny part. Before she had a chance to open the door, my sister-in-law came out with a pan of water and threw it practically over her, and she didn't see her. And all those people on the bank all saw that woman. And most of them from the factory went up to the house. And they went around it; they went everywhere. There wasn't a sight of that woman. And the old lady said, in all her years she never saw a thing like that.

Now the ones that described her, that were closer to her that day on the bank—she was completely in black, very slim, but her face was snow white. There was no recognition in her face at all. They said her face was like paste. And then the priest heard about it. He used to stay at our house when he came from the Bay. He asked the old lady, where did that lady come from. She said, "All I could say, when I saw her coming, is that she came out of the sun." Now that's a funny thing, isn't it? And as yet, there was nothing ever happened.

I'll tell you one thing, and I've asked three clergymen since it happened about it, and I don't know—even you might say I didn't really see it. When my last little boy was born—he's ten years old—I was in Neil's Harbour Hospital. I was reading a western magazine. There was no thought whatsoever in my mind of ghosts or dead people or anything like this—and it seemed like there was something telling me to look up at the door, that there's something watching me. And I looked.

And my husband's father—he had been dead two years—honest to God, that man was standing in the door, looking at me. And a very serious, serious look was on his face. But at the time I didn't get frightened, because it came on me so quick.

109

But it wasn't like I was looking at you. It was like pebbles in front of it, like pebbly glass. And when I blinked my eyes, he was gone. The funny part about that, he wasn't dressed in the same clothes that he went into his grave in. Now, in his grave, he went in a black suit. What he had on was a red checkered shirt and a pair of green dungarees. And his arms were folded like this.

So it was the next morning that it really hit me, that I did get scared. I told the nurse. She asked me what was wrong, so I told her what I had seen. And why should I see that? You know, to see something like that, I thought something was going to happen to the baby. "Well," she said, "did you know that this was the room that he died in?" I said, "No, I didn't."

So when I came home, it bothered me so much, there were three different priests came to this area, and each one of them I asked. Well, the first person, he told me I imagined it. The second clergyman told me that women are always seeing things. And the third told me that if I were ever to see it again, to speak to it and ask him what he wants. But as yet, I haven't seen him since.

Kenneth MacKenzie Tells of Old Cures

MY GRANDMOTHER WAS A MACLEAN. They had had to change their names from Mac-Gregor to MacLean because MacGregors were outlawed in Scotland at that time—so she happened to come here as a MacLean. And I remember her. She was 102, I think, when she died. And her cheeks were as red—when she was over 100. And she had all her teeth. And they told me that she grew a tooth when she was something over 70. And she had a son who had a double set of teeth. And he never lost a tooth, and he was 85 when he died.

But my grandfather—I'll tell you this. Years ago, my grandfather, he was quite a man to swear. Although he was a Presbyterian. But there was one woman, she was very, very religious—and she was bedridden. And she was in a bed right off of the kitchen. And my grandfather went in the house one day and he sat down at the stove, and I guess the language he was using was terrible. And she chastized him for swearing.

"Well," he said, "if you had the same thing wrong with you that I got"—remember, she was bedridden; but he considered his ailment worse—he said, "If you had the same thing wrong with you, you'd be swearing, too."

"Well," she said, "what's wrong?" He said he had a toothache. She said, "Well, if I could get to where I'd want to go with you, I'd cure your toothache." He said, "Where do you want to go?" So she described the place—it was a spring up in the side of a hill, in the side of the mountain, up in the Big Intervale there. And they could see it from where they were.

Well anyway, he said, "I'll see that you get up there."

So it was all feather beds they had. He went home and he took one of those ticks off the bed, and he emptied the feathers out of it and went and put her in this tick, and carried her up the mountain where she wanted to go. And she went through whatever ritual it was—I *did* hear it. It was a prayer that she said, and he had to say it too—and it was in Gaelic they were saying it. And he took a mouthful of water and said a prayer, and she scooped up a sod or he scooped it up, and he spit under the sod and put the sod back.

Well, his toothache disappeared.

But a few years afterward, my mother came home, just before I was born. And she had a toothache. And she wasn't too old at the time, and she complained of this toothache, and my grandfather told her this story about the old lady curing his toothache. She said, "I wish the old lady was here now"—she had died. "Well," he said, "I remember exactly what she did. If you want to go and try it, we'll go."

Well, they went up. I remember my mother talking about it. They had to cross the river on horseback, and she fell off right in the middle of the river. But anyhow, they got up to this spring and they went through the same performance as this old lady did. My mother never had toothache again. And I've never had a toothache in my life. I don't know what toothache means.

And my mother (when she was older) sat on a chair in the kitchen there, and the doctor came and pulled, I think, fifteen teeth, and she didn't even have it frozen. She was quite old when the doctor pulled her teeth. And I've got teeth broken off right to the gum—and I never had a toothache. And this happened through her. I wasn't

born when my grandfather took her up there—
that was just before I was born.

(*And they do say that these things have to be
transmitted from a man to a woman....*)

And from a woman to a man. But those old fellows that came from Scotland, they all had that. And I've often heard the old fellows talking about this same woman—this woman was a MacPherson. All I ever heard them call her was Widow MacPherson. You know, there'd be kids around, and a fellow would get a piece of bark or something in his eye—and then the kids would run up to this old lady and tell her that a certain person had something in his eye. She'd go through some kind of a ritual—the person would probably be miles away—and she'd come up with that piece of bark. They used to say she'd take a cup of water—but nobody knew just what she did—nobody ever saw. She'd go in her room.

Now we were talking about spearing salmon. There was a MacLean woman up there—she had two sons—and her husband was dead for a number of years, and they were having quite a struggle to get along. And they were peeling birchbark—that's what they used to use under shingles, was birchbark—I think they used to get a cent a sheet for it in Cheticamp. So she and the two boys went out and they peeled a lot of this bark, and they hid it in this old Widow MacPherson's house—they didn't hide it, they stored it there. And they had it piled in probably the kitchen, I don't know. And the way they had it weighted down was boards on top and big rocks to keep it flat.

And sometime through the summer, the river filled up with salmon—they had a freshet and salmon came in. And my uncle Rod and a Murray fellow decided to go get some salmon, but they needed something to make a light (for spearing salmon at night). And the only thing they could

113

think of was this birchbark. They decided that if they go and take the bark and pay her for it, she won't have to carry it to Cheticamp.

So they went up to this house, nice sunny afternoon—and they couldn't take a board off of that pile of birchbark. They said, when they'd touch it, the house would shake and you'd think there was a thousand horses galloping around outside. So they didn't take the bark. And they weren't stealing it. They were figuring on paying her for it. But it was well-protected—by something.

They believed very much in witches, in the old country, the old fellows here talked. (*Any talk of witches in the Margaree Valley?*) No. Well, yes, there was an old woman up the Big Intervale there, and a bunch of them were watching her one day, and she threw a chip in the river and jumped on it and crossed over. But I never heard too much of that. Because my folks didn't believe in that sort of thing. (*But you wouldn't consider Widow MacPherson a witch?*) Oh, no. They figured what she had, it was more a gift. It was a gift.

And the same woman, I've heard my grandmother say, there was a MacLeod, a little kid—she used to take epileptic fits—and they got Widow MacPherson. And my grandmother said that she was there with her—she used to take somebody with her, you know, to drive a horse. And she went into this house and asked them where the kid fell for the first fall that she had. And she got a chicken—and I guess it had to be a black chicken—and she took the chicken and put it on her hand and stroked it a few times. And whether she mesmerized it or hypnotized it—anyway, the chicken went to sleep. So she took the chicken and buried it in the basement underneath where the kid fell. The child never had another fit.

A Story from Christmas Island

MY NAME IS HUGH MACKENZIE, a son of the late Archibald MacKenzie and his wife Catherine (née Campbell) who lived at Rear Christmas Island, Cape Breton.

We were a family of ten who were blessed with the gift of being brought up by good God-fearing parents who were living close to God every minute of their daily lives. The family rosary was recited in Gaelic every night at nine o'clock, and to this was added the litany to St. Joseph, the scapular prayers and prayers for the holy souls. No one was allowed to go outside the door in the morning until the morning offering was recited. I mention this so that the reader may visualize the religious practices which were strictly followed in the household where this unusual experience was witnessed by many.

It occurred in December 1907, two days after the late Father J. A. M. Gillis took over as parish priest.

We all retired early as usual. My sister Sarah Catherine, aged nine, and Mary Elizabeth (now Sister Carlotta of the Dominican Order, New York) went to bed together. They had just settled down when a loud rapping started under Sarah Catherine's head. My father and mother who were in the adjoining room could hear it and in a moment we were all on the scene. The holy water was generously sprinkled over the spot where the sound was coming from. The only result was that the rapping came faster and louder.

She was then placed on the bare floor, but the rapping continued. Then we all joined in saying the rosary, and during the reciting of the litany,

115

the response "Have mercy on us" was accompanied by a louder rap.

The next morning my father went to see Father Gillis after Mass. The good priest was very sympathetic, and he told my father to come after him that night. With horse and waggon, I went with Father that evening. When the priest arrived, he blessed the house outside and inside. Then my sister was put to bed and the moment her head touched the pillow, the rapping commenced. Father Gillis put on his stole and started praying and sprinkling holy water, but the rapping continued. I remember him saying, "If that was the devil I'd drive him out quick, but it must be some poor neglected soul who is looking for help." He also advised to be saying prayers and offering masses and he was sure the rapping would cease.

The next evening my sister was moved to a bedroom that was off the living room. The rapping started and my father went in. He came out in a few seconds and told us that he saw a beautiful white hand rapping at her head. He went for the priest at once and on arrival the priest looked in to her room. He turned and said, "Sure enough, I saw that beautiful hand. It must be an angel for I never saw a hand like it."

The neighbors used to call in every evening to see and hear what was taking place. I remember one evening in particular when my Uncle Hector, Neil V. MacNeil, Anthony MacKenzie and several more were present. They were all gathered in the room and the rapping was coming very loud and the pillow under her head was moving up and down with every rap. I looked in on the door and on seeing the pillow moving I shouted, "Work away you b____r." All of a sudden the pillow went flying from under her head across the room and hit me on the chest. I got such a fright that I had what was known as the "yellow jaundice" (known in Gaelic as "tinneas buidhe") for two weeks.

This rapping went on for about a week. Then one evening as she was sitting in a rocking chair in front of the kitchen stove, we were all startled to hear her singing the litany of the Blessed Virgin in Latin. We looked at her and she appeared to be in a trance. On finishing the litany she started calling us all by name and pleading to come with her, that Saint Mary Magdalen was leading her around to see the sights.

Then she started talking as if she was having interviews with people who died long before she was born. The first one she met was Teresa MacKenzie, wife of her grand uncle Donald MacKenzie. I may add here that Teresa died many years before she was born. I well remember her raising her hands and joyfully saying, "Here comes Teresa Little Donald." She had quite a conversation with her. And then she would name out others as she was meeting them and she would be giving them news about their descendants here on earth.

As the trance was coming to a close she appeared to be suffering a terrible agony. It seemed as if she did not want to come back to earth again. She was pleading with Saint Mary Magdelen to let her stay with her. Before she revived we feared she would choke. She was as if having a convulsion.

When it was all over, she told us that she saw herself being carried away to such a beautiful place and she was calling us all as she did not want to leave us behind. Then she related her conversation with Teresa and that Teresa told her to tell Mairi Bhan, her daughter, that there was a ring in an old chest in an upstairs room and for Mairi Bhan to look for it and give it to her and she could wear it. Mairi Bhan was sent for and on being informed, she went to search for the ring. She failed to find it and the next evening while in another trance, she met Teresa again and she told her that the ring was among some papers in the corner of the trunk and she could find it there.

117

Another search was made and the ring was found. It was too large a size for her finger and a string was tied to it and up around her wrist.

I am not going to enumerate the names of all the people or souls she met except that she had quite a talk with her grandparents whom she had never seen. There was something she had never heard of, that there was a stillborn child in Uncle Hector's family, and she shouted while in a trance, "Look at Uncle Hector's little boy, he has no name." He was baptized at birth. She often while in a trance would say, "Look at the poor people in purgatory, some of them are almost out of it."

At that time there was a man, James MacLean, "Sheumas Dhomhnuil Gilleasbuig Chalum," on his death bed. He lived a few miles out the glen. In a trance one evening she shouted, "Look at Jim MacLean coming; he died." My father said to check the time and it was twenty to eight. At eleven o'clock, a neighbor, Archie D. MacKenzie, came and he said that he was sorry he could not come earlier as he was out at MacLean's and that Jim had died. My father asked him what time did he die. He said he died at twenty to eight.

Father Gillis, after watching her in a trance, suggested to move her in to the Glebe House. She was there for a few months and attended school as a normal child. I do not know if there was any recurrence at the Glebe House, but I was told that many priests visited there to see her. Father Gillis advised never to mention the subject to her again and nobody ever did.

THIS ACCOUNT was written out by Hugh MacKenzie on March 27th, 1967, at the request of his younger brother, Archie Alex, who felt that this family story should be carefully preserved by someone who was actually there. A version of this story was told by Dan MacNeil as "A Story of Christmas Island" in Issue Number 6, *Cape Breton's Magazine*.

118

John Reppa: Mystery at Blackett's Lake

MY NAME IS JOHN STEPHEN REPPA. I was born in Weston, Ontario. However, my family is originally from here. They are Polish immigrants. They moved here at the turn of the century. Whereupon, they lived in the Pier, worked in the steel plant. I was born in Ontario because my father moved there to have some work. They moved back when I was about three, and I've been living here ever since. I'm thirty years old....

(Why don't you just simply tell me the story.)

It started for me—I believe it was in 1977, in the very early spring, in February. I was seventeen years old, I think, at the time. And, (it) started at Blackett's Lake. Where me and a friend of mine whose name is Lawrence—who doesn't like talking about this—refuses to talk about this with me to this day. I can't find him any more, anyway—he's out West somewhere.

However, we were out there one particular night, because my family has a bungalow on the Blackett's Lake. And his sister lived there as well. We were going to an East Bay dance—a teenage dance. And we had picked up a pint of rum at his sister's house. And we were going to go take it to the dance. But on leaving, we thought that it was a bad idea, because there were always police roadblocks out there.

So as we left his sister's house, we went—if you're familiar with the lake and its area, you'll know there's a little bridge where it connects with the Sydney River. As we were leaving the lake area, we crossed that bridge and stopped. Now at that time, there weren't any houses or anything around there. There was just darkness, and a ditch on one side of the road, beach on the other.

So on the other side of this road, there was a large clear ditch, with a bunch of small alder trees growing out. And that time of year, the crust on the snow was fairly thick and fairly hard. You could walk on it without falling through. And around all the alder trees, there was an area of I'd say about five inches across, that went straight down, from the surface down. It was like a clear area away from the trunk of the tree.

Now, away from all the other alders in a large clear area, there was this one particular alder tree that was all alone and far away from the others. He saw it, I saw it, we both knew where it was. Upon seeing that, we decided to lay this bottle of rum—not to take with us—halfway in this hole, and halfway out. So it was just halfway in and halfway out, right where you could see it.

There was nobody living out there; nobody saw us out there. It was the middle of winter, there was nobody staying in the bungalows that were on the far side, away from it. There was nobody near there.

So, we left. We went to the dance, we had a nice evening, we left. We go back to my house in Sydney River. The Late Show is coming on, and Lawrence suggests that we go out to the lake— this is getting on to one o'clock or two o'clock in the morning. (He) suggests that we go out to the lake, pick up the bottle of rum—pint—and bring it back to my place. And we'll have some drinks and watch the Late Show.

So we get in his car—he had a small yellow Vega—and we drive out to the lake. And we pull up next to the spot where we put it. And we get out, and of course the bottle's gone. Right where we left it—it's gone, disappeared. And we knew nobody saw us there—we knew that for a fact, because there was just nobody out there, it was pitch black. But we could see where we left it, because it was just this one little tree, far away from the other little ones.

So, I go up to the hole, he goes up to the hole, we're sticking our hands right down around the trunk of the tree, trying to feel right down to the grass. Couldn't feel it—it wasn't down there. So, we couldn't quite figure this out. So we decided to start searching all the other trees, just on the off chance that we'd made a mistake and put it in one of the other trees. Although we knew we put it in this other one. We couldn't believe that it was gone.

So we started to search. So we're going around all these trees, and we're sticking our hands down about a foot and a half down, right to the grass, through all this hard-packed snow. Nothing. Nothing. We went around.

Lawrence said, "This is ridiculous. We know we put it here." So, this is what we decided to do. He took his car and turned it right into the ditch, and put his high beams right on that tree. Then we started to wrestle out this huge snow shovel. Because this is what we figured had happened: we figured that it fell down to the grass, and it slid out underneath the snow somewhere. That's all we could figure could happen. So we start to wrestle out this big snow shovel. It took us a good, almost, five minutes to get it out, because it was a big, ungainly shovel, and it was a small little car.

So we got it out. We walked over to the tree. And I'm sure, just as he was going to swing up, this is when we heard this scream.

Now this scream wasn't like anything you've ever heard in your life. This scream started out so high-pitched and abrasive that—it sort of sounded like tires being squealed on a really sharp turn or something. Only really higher pitched than that.

So we stopped, we froze—we just froze dead solid, because we didn't know what this noise was. I sort of looked up the road towards where Route 4 would be, because I sort of thought it might have been tires squealing. But, it began to drop in pitch. And it got lower and lower and lower. We started to realize that it was a sort of a voice of some sort—a real abrasive and horrible voice, too, I'm going to tell you. You've never heard nothing like this. And it dropped in pitch. And then it dawned upon us that it wasn't coming from any particular direction at all. It seemed to be reverberating all around us. And this went on for a long time, like about fifteen seconds it took for this scream to go down in pitch. And it ended off getting really low, like a low gutteral growl, sort of really horrible. "Blaaaahhh," sort of thing. And then it just stopped dead. And echoed off the hills for a second or two. And there we were, fro-zen—just frozen solid. And didn't know what was going on. Scared white.

It took us about two seconds to get that shovel back into the car, and pshhh—gone—out of there.

Well, the next day, I got my uncle to drive me out. I didn't know what had happened. I thought that maybe somebody was murdered, or God only knows what—it was the most horrible sound I've ever heard in my life. And so I said, "If you see police around or anything, don't stop. For God's sake. I don't know what happened here."

But there was nobody around. I got him to stop. Exactly where we had stopped. And of course, the pint of rum was sitting halfway in the hole and halfway out, in the exact same tree, ex-actly like we left it the night before.

And so, that was the end of my story with this. But that really intrigued me for a long, long time. Because the screech—the howl—whatever you want to call it—I heard—wasn't like anything that was on.... I knew—when you heard it, you knew it wasn't from something on the face of the earth. I'm telling you this.

So, it's really terrifying. I get nervous just talking about it. But for years and years it's sort of, you know, something eating at the back of your head. You know, you forget about it—"Was that ever weird!" You're a teenager, so your mind wanders away on other things as the years go by. However, after high school, I started to think, you know, this is really strange—a really strange thing that happened to me.

So I started asking around about people who go out there, and live out there. I'm starting to pick up a lot of really interesting stories. But it eventually led me here, to the Beaton Institute (at University College of Cape Breton). Where I found out that the original Blackett family had—they were the first white settlers here—they had almost the exact same experience.

In the sense that things were moved, and the next morning—or, things were okay, they come back the next day, things were moved, things reappeared. And also, the terrible howl, which is a real link....

(*So you told me you started to talk to people. And what was the response you were getting from it?*) Now here's a real interesting thing I found, is that it always seemed to be teenagers that were having these things. More than anything else. And in fact, I was a teenager at the time.

And I've had people say that, more than anything, that they've seen a lot of strange lights out there—flying over the lake, flying over the ice at

night. That's the most common thing I get from
people. Although some people have said they've
been followed around in the area there with what
appeared to be—someone once told me it was
something like a Christmas-tree-shape thing. It
was dark in the winter, and all they could think of
was a shape of a Christmas tree, or a pyramid-
sort-of-shape thing, following them across a field,
and stuff. A black Christmas tree sort of shape.

(*Anything else?*) There's been—here's something I want to confirm. Although I can't do it for
sure. I don't know what the real story is. There's
been a few kind of strange deaths happening
around the lake....

But the most strange one I heard was when I
was about fifteen. And this was before anything
happened to me. I just thought it was a weird sort
of drowning that happened here. There's some
people out there that had a bungalow out there.
And I believe it was their son that found the body
of this girl that had drowned there. Apparently—
what he told my brother—is that the police had
told them that the girl that they found drowned in
the lake was from Ontario. She wasn't related to
anybody here. She had never been here before in
her life. She didn't know anybody that lived here.
She didn't know anybody here at the time. She'd
apparently caught a plane from Ontario to the
Sydney Airport, took a taxi to the lake, and
drowned herself. And this is what he told.

(*So now, you are researching anything that says
"Blackett."*) I've been looking for this. There's not
too much around. But it didn't occur to me till the
other day that I should start looking under "Cox-
heath" and "Coxheath Mountain," which leads
right down to the lake. And what clued me into
this was that I was completing a hunter's safety
course. And the instructor had told me that—we
were doing a map-and-compass training—and he
said you can't always rely on your compass. For

instance, I know many people who go up on Cox-heath Mountain and have their compasses spinning like crazy when they get up there. Which I assume to be—which they assume to be—from the mineral and metal deposits, which I believe actually are under there. So it very well could be that. And I'm not outside of saying that all these strange lights that people are seeing might have something to do with metal deposits causing some sort of bizarre ball lightning or something. You know, it could be a good explanation for all of this. However, I don't know. But I do know it's been happening for a long time.

I'm glad, actually, that somebody does want to make a record of it. Because I hate to live my life and die, and nobody know about this. Kind of interesting to see it get written down.

A Story Fr. John Angus Rankin Did Not Refute

It's the same as what I tell people about ghost stories. Maybe seventy per cent of them you can charge up to a person's emotional make-up at the time. But there are too many, that there's no way in God's earth that you can refute it. And when you know that person, and know that they're truthful, and—as a matter of fact, they'd be afraid to make it up—what is their gain, except to tell the thing as they experienced it?

See, I remember, oh, in 1945, my last year in seminary—I was collecting for *The Casket* paper. And I did it by bike, starting in Hawkesbury right down through to the end of Inverness County. And this particular night I landed at a certain place. I knew the woman—she was a great friend of my mother's, although my mother lived in Inverness and she lived in this end of the county. So I spent the night there.

And it happened to be a kind of a rainy day. I landed in the afternoon. So she made me slip my clothes and go to bed for awhile, and dry my clothes. And in the evening the neighbours knew *The Casket* agent was around—that's what they called you at that time. So here was kind of a curious being—he was going to be ordained next year, and people wanted to meet this young man, find out what was going on in the county— because you travelled the whole county. And of course ghost stories would come in from time to time.

So at that time, I didn't believe in a ghost. (*1945. So you personally had had no experiences then.*) No. I had experiences, but I was forced to face them—and it was (always) something natural.

So, we'll say there were seven or eight men in, and she was working around, and could listen to every story. And I could refute every one of them. I'd ask, "Well, did you stay to investiage?" "Well no, as soon as I saw this, I knew who it was." I said, "You *thought* you knew." They said, "Yeah. I just left and ran." So then I'd say, "Well, I was in a similar situation and I couldn't run. I had to face it. And it was something natural...."

So after they left, she said, "You did a great job tonight. A lot of people went home feeling that, well, maybe they didn't see anything. Since you're so good," she said, "try this one."

She said, "I married my husband. I came to live here. His mother was dead, and he was living alone for two years. And one night I was out at the woodpile, taking in firewood for the morning of the next day. I was down on my knees, I loaded up my arms, I raised my eyes—and I saw this woman in front of me. I never saw that woman before; I didn't know her. But I saw the kind of a dress she had, and everything else. I got scared. But," she said, "the house was just a little piece away, and I went in the house and forgot about her."

"Then," she said, "oh, about two months later we were finishing haymaking. And one of the neighbours came over to help my husband. I was out with them working all day. So we were putting in the last load of hay. And when we came to the barn the men said, 'You go in and get supper. We'll pitch the load ourselves, and we'll go in and have supper.' And I went down to the house, took two buckets, went down to the well to get some water. Filled the buckets, turned around. And the woman I had seen before at the woodpile walked all the way from the spring to the house with me."

She said, "I fainted." She said, "I don't know how long I was out, but the men coming in found me. I was pregnant at the time, and they thought that I had worked too much in the sun. So they picked me up and brought me in. I didn't say a word to anyone.

"Two weeks later," she said, "my husband was down in Port Hood. And he was coming home. And just turning in the lane, the horses saw something, and he saw something. Horses bolted and ran away on him. The barn stopped them. He was thrown out of the wagon and he broke three ribs. So we had the doctor, and he strapped him up, and he was convalescing at the time.

"So I decided I was going to clean the attic. I hadn't cleaned it since I took over the new home. So," she said, "I went up. And going through her trunks, I saw a picture, a frolic. And there were ten women with spinning wheels. And in the centre of the group was the one I saw at the woodpile and at the well.

"I brought it down and I put it on the table. And my husband came to dinner, and he picked up the picture and he said, 'Where'd you find this?' 'Oh,' I said, 'I was doing some housecleaning upstairs.' I said, 'I ran across this, and I don't know who they are.' 'Oh,' he said, 'you don't know any of them.' He said, 'They're all dead. This is Mrs. MacIsaac, and this is Mrs. MacCormack, and this is Mrs. MacDonald, and this is Mrs. Rankin, and this is Mrs. Beaton, and so on. And the one in the centre, that's my mother.'"

She said, "She was the one I saw at the woodpile and at the well." She said, "After that, I didn't stay in the house alone. No matter where he went, I went.

"So," she said, "we went down home, to your part of the country, for Hallowe'en. And my hus-

128

band had butchered some animals and took them down. We were selling them, getting groceries for the winter, and all that. So we had decided we'll stay at home in Inverness that night. And friends gathered in, there was a violin player. And we had fuarag (a mixture of cold water or cold milk and meal) and we had stepdancing, and we had sets. Lunchtime came.

"So my mother sent me out to the outhouse there. It was a bright night in October. The moon was just full and you wouldn't even need a light or anything. And I took a pitcher to get some milk and cream, and a dish for the butter. I filled the pitcher, I filled the dish with butter, turned around. The woman was standing in front of me, at the door. I'm blocked. I said, 'What in the name of God do you want?'

"'Well,' she said, 'I tried to talk to you twice. I tried to talk to your huband once.' She said, 'I promised $4.00 for Masses for my son when he was very sick, so that God would save him and leave him with me.' She said, 'You're married to him now. I never paid that money.' She said, 'You go to some priest tomorrow and give them $4.00, and I won't bother you or anybody else.'

"Now. How do you refute that?"

See, there's a sequel to that. I was a visitor. And these old homes had bedrooms off the parlour. It's something like this. You've got a parlour here, and you've got a bedroom right in there, eh? So I was put to bed—no electricity—with a lamp. And by the time I had finished my prayers, the sparks were coming out of the wick, indicating very little oil. And I wasn't too bloody brave—I'll tell you God's truth—at this stage of the game. And I knew that if anybody died, they'd likely die in the bed that I was in, and the wake would be out in the next room. Which added to the situation!

They had a verandah the length of the house. So I blew the lamp out, and I pulled the clothes over my head, and I started trying to sleep. And I'm just dozing off, and I heard walking across the verandah—over, back, over, and back.

Well, my heart didn't stop, but it went pretty close to it. I reached down and got my pants and pulled it up and found the—I had matches—and lit the lamp. And just when I was about halfway across the room, the walking was going in the opposite direction. So I went over and I pulled over the shade. Couldn't see a thing. And the lamp went out. I got back to my bed fast. Put it on the floor alongside of the bed.

I was just getting ready to yell out to the people in the other end of the house to come down because, I said, the old lady's not finished, she wants to see somebody else. I heard, "Baaa!" It was a pet lamb. And the pet lamb was walking right from end to end of the verandah. And you'd swear to God it was a woman's shoes walking. And if that lamb hadn't bleated, I'd have left there saying, "What was the noise?" And, "That house is haunted." But the lamb bleated, and then I knew right away what it was.

A fellow's still scared.

Mary Ann MacDougall on Seeing a Droke

WE WERE OUT DANCING ONE NIGHT, me and my husband, and when we came out to the door, ready for home, he said to me, "Come and have a look at this. I've often heard you say you've never seen a droke."

Well, I had good eyesight then. And it was coming this way, and it was going right queer, making a funny noise. It was up a good piece but still you could hear it. (*Mary Ann made a sound: a kind of a hissing sound, a whoosh.*) Yeah, some kind of a sound. It was going anyway, over toward the church. And I think it was the next day we heard of a death—I forget now, it was so long—it was only a young child that died. And it's buried over there in that graveyard, in the same place that light went toward.

Then your brother, Gabe, fell off a truck and was killed. At the age of seventeen, wasn't it, Gabe, your brother (died)? And I don't know how long it was before he died, before this happened—it might have been three weeks—that he saw his own droke. He saw the light. And this is how I always believed and I always will till I die—that there are foretokens.

Because he came in that night, he came right in the front door, he came in in an awful hurry. He opened the door right wide. We were in bed. And we had our bed downstairs. And I'll never forget. We had a trunk. He sat on a trunk. Gabe, I don't know but you remember that trunk. And he said, "Are you asleep, Mama?" And I said, "No." He said, "Did you see anything, did you see

131

a light?" And I said, "No, dear." And just as the word came out of his mouth he said, "Awww"— like that, and away he went into a faint.

My poor husband jumped up ahead of me and he grabbed the water and he went in and got a rag and washed his face with it. And I jumped up, half crazy. So anyway, when we got him back to himself again, he just sat in that same place—and we asked him what happened. He said, "A light. A light gave me that fright. I was coming home and there was a light ahead of me." He said, "It passed over me. It kept going."

Now that's what you call a droke.

"And it went to pieces right at our upper gate...."

So, oh, we didn't know what in the name of God to say. Begin thinking this and thinking that. So, that passed on all right.

About three weeks after that, maybe a month, there was a picnic here in Ingonish and he went with the rest of the boys. And on his way coming home, the dear fellow fell off of the truck and was killed. And when they brought him home, his re- mains were laid right at the upper gate. That's as true as I've got God to meet with. They left him there to come down to break the news to us....

The Haunted Railroad Car

THE HAUNTED CAR STORY. One summer the Cape Breton Railroad Company decided to fence their railroad property from St. Peters to Point Tupper. So they sent a man and his son, and an old man for company, from George's River with a work car to live in while they were getting the job done. The work car was put on a siding at Whiteside. The railroad foreman, Alfred Morrison, ordered a flanger car to be put on the same siding the boss's car was on.

From St. Peters to Sporting Mountain, we walked to our work. The section foreman got lumber and got the boys to build bunks and shelves to store our food and dishes. While the flanger car was in St. Peters, the boss who was doing the job got news from his home that some relative or friend died, so he went back to his home and took his son and the old man with him. After they were gone and the flanger car was moved to the same siding that the boss's car was put on, we started to work during the day.

One night some of the boys went to a dance in Louisdale. They took a pump car that we had and travelled to the dance which was about twelve miles from where our car was. So one of our boys made a dish of fudge and we played cards until eleven o'clock, after which we went to bed.

Everything was quiet until we heard the boys coming home from the dance, singing. I suppose they had a few drinks of liquor and felt happy. They took the pump car off the main line and put it on the siding. Then this big object appeared before them, so tall they couldn't see the head. The boys froze right where they were, too frightened

133

to speak. They made a dash for the car we were in and when we opened the door they fell face first on the floor. The next day it was the talk of the place.

The third night, one of the hired men, Dan Thibeau, said to all of us, "There is no such thing as ghosts. I'll prove that to you tonight." So we left it at that, and waited for our brave man to perform his magic. We all went to bed early because we were tired after our day's work on the fence. So just at twelve o'clock, we all were awakened from the noise on the roof of the car. It sounded like a big stone was rolling from one end of the car to the other. One fellow got up out of bed and lighted all the kerosene lamps. Our magic man picked up a switch broom that was near the bunk we were in. This kind of a broom has a sharp steel point on one end and a broom on the other, used on (railway track) switches to break ice and sweep it away. He held the broom in his hand and shouted, "Whoever in hell you are, I dare you to come in this car."

With that, the bolt that was on the door and a button, started to turn and the door started to open. The two Morrison boys braced their feet on the door trying to keep it shut but their legs buckled. The door opened wide and this big creature all in white clothes floated down to the other door and disappeared.

Our brave boy held the broom in his hand but never tried to use it on the ghost. He turned towards me and said, "You are going to sleep alone tomorrow night. I'm going to sleep with one of the other boys. I think he is after you." I felt the cold chills creeping over me. What if it should happen? What would I do? I had to face it.

So sure enough that ghost came in the car the fourth night and threw pots, pans, dishes and food on the floor. Then it came towards me, put its ice cold hand on my neck and started to

134

squeeze. I screamed from fright so it let go and disappeared. I stayed awake the rest of the night.

The boss and his son and the old man came back from George's River, so we were all telling them our story of what happened. Well, the boss laughed so much that the tears were running down his cheeks. "Well," he said, "this job is not very good for you people in the wilderness. You could finish up landing in an asylum." As far as he was concerned we were crazy. We walked away and let him have his fun. Maybe he was right, time would tell.

So that night we went to bed early and enjoyed our sleep until some time through the night we were awakened by someone hammering on the door. One of our boys went and opened the door. Here was the boss in his underwear with a lamp in his hand, pale as a ghost, shivering from fright, and his son behind him. "My God," he said, "our car was picked up about thirty feet in the air and dropped back down on the rails. The old man was thrown out of his bunk onto the floor, he is still unconscious. The rest of us landed on the floor." We said, "What happened? You don't believe in ghosts! There is no one here that could lift a box-car." He said, "Tomorrow will be your last day here. I know you need the job and the money but I will never want to live in a place like that."

So the last day of work I walked fifteen miles to a friend's place. He was pogy fishing in the United States. I slept with one of his boys that night. I guess he didn't get much sleep, no doubt I must have been restless. I heard from the people that our boys (back at the work site) put on a party, invited the young girls and boys and a violin player. They danced for awhile and were having a good time until Mr. Ghost took over and he rocked that car from side to side so hard that they were all falling over each other. They were so frightened that they had to accompany each other to their homes.

After I got home I was talking to the section foreman. He told me the whole story. Even some young kids broke into the car and tried to steal whatever was of any value to them but apparently Mr. Ghost beat them to it. When he showed up they went home screaming and dropped everything they had taken.

The section foreman told me that the flanger he was using was taken from Harbour Boucher. They used it there behind the plow to clear the railroad yard. The reason it was taken off and put on the Cape Breton line was that a man got killed operating it. The section foreman said that the end of the car that the man had been killed on was abandoned and the same kind of a rig was put on the opposite end of the car. It seems that the flange was operated by a lever that had two guard rails on both sides to keep it up off the track. There were holes on both side of the guard rails and a pin was put through to keep the flange up at night. Leaving Point Tupper before or after a snow storm, he had to operate this flanger. He would get the car turned around because that man's spirit was still on his job. He said he was nervous at first to see him there, but he got used to it!

"THE HAUNTED RAILROAD CAR" is from a manuscript by Stephen Patrick Sampson. It is part of a much longer life history Mr. Sampson prepared with his granddaughter Leona Hussey, which was a prizewinner in the *Cape Breton's Magazine* Local History Contest, 1990.

Mickey MacNeil Tells of the Priest Who Owed a Mass

THERE WAS A CHURCH—I just don't know whether it was on the other side, Boularderie side, or out St. Peters—it doesn't matter. There was a church. And now, many's the time we find fault with young people being bad. You know, there'll be a little harm in them, they'll be doing little things. But we have no control—we do not know God's plan. We do not know His plan, what He has planned.

But anyhow, this little boy, this young boy, was a little bit bad. Well, maybe more than a little bit bad. He used to steal the money out of the poor box, out of the box at the church. But everything, too, has a purpose, you never know. So, anyway, the priest caught on that he was taking—the money was going. And they pinned it on him. And he was the fellow that was taking the money, this young fellow. So the priest said to him, "You have to now," he said, "stay three nights in the church, as punishment, alone."

Well, there is no place more lonelier than to be in a church all night by yourself, from sunset until sunrise in the morning.

So the first night he spent there. And he was quite frightened. But he stayed in the back seat. But he couldn't get out—the doors were locked. So at twelve, exactly twelve, a priest came to the altar. Well, at those times—and long after—Mass could not be said until after twelve, 'cause you'd have to be in daylight—you could not say Mass in the afternoon. It would have to be in the morning. And it couldn't be until after 12 again.

137

So the lights, the candles, they lit up. (*They lit up.*) Oh, yes, they lit up. (*By themselves.*) By themselves. Priest came to the altar. And the priest turned around, and he asked, "Is there anybody," he said, "here, that can serve the Mass?" That would mean an altar boy. The boy didn't say a word—he was too scared. So the priest vanished, or disappeared.

The next night, he came—the boy was in. At twelve o'clock the priest came again. But the boy was up a little further, more handier to the centre. The priest hollered, asked, was there anybody that would serve Mass with him. Candles were all lighted. No, there wasn't anybody. Lights went, disappeared, and the priest went.

The (parish) priest met the young fellow (after) the second night. "You've got another night," he said. "I hope it'll teach you a lesson, too." The young fellow never said a word.

But the third night, the boy went up to the front, to the front seat. Priest came out, just sharp, a minute after twelve. All the candles lighted. He asked, "Is there anybody here that'll serve the Mass?" "I will!" he said—the boy. "Come up," he said. And the boy got at the foot of the altar. The priest started the Mass. Finished the Mass, the boy was with him.

So the priest turned to him and he said, "Boy," he said, "I'm coming here 50 years," he said, "and I have nobody," he said, "to answer the Mass, until tonight. Now," he said, "I'm on my way to Heaven. There's nothing to hold me out of Heaven," he said, "I completed—I made the Mass."

So, the first fellow that met him in the morning was the parish priest that was after putting him in. "Now," he said, "that," he said, "'ll teach you, young fellow," he said, "a lesson. You won't be so anxious to go in the church again." Well, the young fellow being mad, cross, he turned to the priest. "Well, Father," he said, "that's all right. But Father," he said, "I know one thing," he said. "I've done one thing," he said, "that you have never done. That is," he said, "I sent a priest to Heaven last night. And you haven't done that yet!"

So the priest then got kind of inquisitive, you know. They questioned him to the point. And I guess when they questioned him to the point, why, the young fellow was right. Everything pointed to there wasn't any mistake. That was one story supposed to be correct, anyway. That's the way with ghosts, and with people.

(*Do you remember where you first heard about that?*) Oh, dear, dear, I guess maybe it would be my grandmother that was telling me—my grandmother that used to talk that first, yeah. My mother then had it. Yeah, those are old stories and things—old priests, you know. The things at those times weren't like today. No, everything is after changing. Yes, everything is after changing, yeah. (*You weren't that little boy, were you?*) No, dear, no! I wasn't that lucky! *Laughter.*

(*Ah, you would see that as lucky.*) Oh, yes. Oh, dear, I feel that, yeah. Of course, I shouldn't—I know, that's all right for me to say. But now, I have no fear of the dead, dear. I have no fear of the dead. I'd have more fear—more fear of the living, if I thought I was in an area that was rough, what we call rough. Areas that were—you know, where there wasn't the very best going on. But of the dead I'd have no fear at all. No, no fear at all. (*I don't know any reason why a person should.*) Certainly no fear at all, no, no.

But if you ran into the dead, you're supposed to address them the way that we learned from our parents to address them. You should ask them, "In the name of God, what do you want? Or what can I do for you? Tell me." But there'll be no obli-

139

gation put before you that's hard or impossible to do. Because they wouldn't do it. There'd be nothing like that happening. Might be only something very simple. Might be only something very simple, that would be asked to be done. (*Again, very merciful.*) Oh, yes, oh, yeah.

Lexie O'Hare & Shake-and-Bake

AND HERE THIS PAST WINTER, just a year ago, I discovered the Shake-and-Bake they had in the stores, you know—for chicken. I suppose you use it and have it. So I'd cook a chicken every week, sometimes twice a week—cook it up, bake it in the oven, put this Shake-and-Bake on it.

So I took this terrible itch, went crazy, tearing myself to pieces. Somebody said, "You always have bacon and eggs for breakfast—it's the bacon, cut out the bacon." I cut out the bacon. I cut out the eggs. And I was very fond of cream cheese—I cut out the cream cheese. I cut out everything, and the itch lasted.

So here, about two months ago, I went to bed, fell asleep. I woke up—and I was in the house I was born in in The Glen. And it was just as it was the day Mother and I were the last two to leave....

But I didn't come in the front door. There was a pantry and flour barrels and things, and stairways going upstairs. I came that way. And the front door was like that. And all this side of that was solid people, so happy, laughing.

140

And we had a sink—it was a wooden sink, you know—and there was a bench—we used to keep an extra bucket of water there. And this bench was there. There was one person sitting on that bench. She was dressed quite young, different to the others.

And I stood looking at the happy people—and they were so happy and so, just, entertaining to one another.

But this one on the bench rose and stood up and walked over to me, and she said, "You know, it's the Shake-and-Bake you're putting on your chicken that's giving you this itch." Everything vanished, just like that.

I cut off the Shake-and-Bake—no more itch.

The next day, visiting with Lexie again, she said she was glad that we had talked about the Shake-and-Bake story. When she went to bed afterwards, she realized that it wasn't her sister Mary who had given the information; it was a little girl she had known in the States.

Lexie: They had this little girl. They were a very, very nice couple—the father and mother—it was marriage formed for them. She never met him until she met him in the States—you know, they pick their wives for them—the gentleman's father and mother. And he married a very lovely Jewish girl. And I got acquainted with them. We were wonderful friends.

And they had a little girl, and she was born with club feet. Dear little thing, they used to bring her into the store to see me. And I fell in love with her and she fell in love with me. She'd be wanting to come in to see Lexie and they'd take her in.

So they had different operations on her feet— feet kept turning back.

141

There was a place in Colorado where they were promised a cure. But they needed money and they didn't have the money. But I loaned them the money to send the child there. And the operation was successful and the feet stayed straight.

One morning they went up—she didn't get up at her usual time—and they found her dead in bed. It was too much strain on the heart, all those operations.

You know, I never forgot that child. I still see her plain as when she used to come in the store.

Willy Pat Fitzgerald

NOW I HAD A SAWMILL pretty close to the house. And there was a Petrie fellow in Middle Harbour, and he and I were terrible good friends. We worked a lot together. And he was sick. He had cancer of the spine. He got punched on a knot hauling logs out at my place. He was sitting on a log coming out of the woods on a Saturday evening, and the mare he had—it was bare ground—she was awful wicked. She used to go fast, you know. And the sleigh hit a windfall that was across the road and jumped like that—and when he came down, he came down on a little sharp knot that was in the log and it punched him right at the end of his tailbone. Turned to cancer and killed him.

And I used to go to see him pretty often. One night I was sitting up with him and he had an awful whisker. It was a Saturday night, the first night I sat up with him. And it was so severe, if you moved him you'd hear him screeching at the road. Well, if he layed right quiet it wasn't too

142

bad. So he asked me coming on morning would I do something for him. And I said, "You bet your life I'll do something for you, if it's in my life to do it." He said, "I'd love for you to shave me."

Well, first I had to clip him. He hadn't shaved for a long time. I got the comb and the scissors and I clipped him. And I got him pillowed up kind of in the bed and I cut his hair. And I shaved him and I washed him. His wife put all clean clothes on him and he looked great. And he told me he felt 90% better. And then, he asked me, "Do you have any wide boards at the mill?" I said, "I haven't any wide boards sawed out but I have logs there that would make wide boards." He said, "I want you to saw out casket boards for me." I said, "Mr. Petrie, are you gone crazy?" "No, be thunders"—that was a word he had—he said, "I know I'm going to need them before long. And if you'll saw them out for me I'll know where to tell them to go get them."

So now the mill I was using I had bought it from him after he got sick. So I went over one morning—I was going to saw—I had a big log rolled in on the skid. And that's what was in my mind—to saw those casket boards for Johnny Petrie. But the way I felt about this, I was going to try to do this underhanded to the Almighty. Johnny wasn't dead then. And I used to make a lot of boxes for dump carts and you needed boards about 12 inches wide for that, for the sides of the dump cart boxes. And there was a fellow wanting me in Dingwall to make him a dump cart box. Well, this is what I decided—that I would saw the log for to have the Almighty think I was sawing it for the cart box, but I was really sawing it to have those boards ready for Johnny Petrie's casket. Because the way I felt about it, if I was sawing this log for casket boards then I was going a step ahead of the Almighty. The Almighty knew more about when Johnny Petrie was going to die than I did. That's the way I felt about it.

And then just before I went to the mill, somebody came and told me Johnny Petrie had died last night. I went to the mill for to saw the log. I slabbed the log—12 inches—and I started. I took off a few first that there was quite a bit of wind on. Well, when the saw came in and she was cutting the square part of the stick—she was cutting the 12 inches. Now, you might think that I'm adding something to this, but the Almighty is my judge and if I'm lying he might hit me dead here. Every board that fell from that saw split from one end to the other. Every board. I don't know, I think it was 3 or 4 boards. After I got into the square part of the log. Every board split from one end to the other, and the log was 12 feet long. I sawed in to about the middle of the log and I went in and shut the engine off and went home.

My wife asked me what was wrong. I said, "Nothing." She said, "There is. You look awful." I said, "About what I have over at the mill. I bought the mill from Johnny Petrie and he died last night—and I feel I should have thought enough of him to have left it shut off today." She said, "That's not hurting Johnny Petrie." But I kind of felt in my own mind I shouldn't have had the mill going. So I quit at that. And the log remained on the carriage I don't know for how long. But after everything was over—they never came to my house for those casket boards; I don't know where they got them but they never came to my place—I guess Johnny never told them to come to me—I went to the mill awhile after and I started up the motor and I pushed the log up to the saw. I sawed the boards off. Every board that fell from the saw—there never was a crack in them. But the three I sawed for Johnny Petrie's casket—that I was going to fool the Almighty, that I was sawing for cart boards—every board I had cut had split in half. Now the log was perfect. There wasn't a rent of any kind in it. It was a red spruce and it was a beautiful log.

Playing Cards

I'VE ACTUALLY SEEN (*Simon Fraser told us*)—well, I've heard it. This is a true story. We were living in Pleasant Bay, way down at what they'd call the Lower End at that time. And there was a bunch of us came to our house that night, to play cards. *Eddie Fraser:* It was on a Sunday, wasn't it?

Simon: Well, it was on a Sunday night, yes. And oh, it must have been about twelve o'clock when they all left. So we got ready and we all went to bed. And after we went to bed—well, we had been playing in the kitchen. We had taken the chairs away from the table after we were through. And after we went to bed we heard the chairs, someone dragging them over to the table, and they started dealing the cards, fancy dealing.

Eddie: I remember that.... We all got up, every one of us.

Simon: This was going on for awhile. Something's going on there, someone's playing cards. We got up and looked around. The chairs were the same way, the cards were the same way as we left them. Couldn't see anyone near them, not a thing. (*Did you talk to one another about this?*) Oh yes. Same time. Everybody in the house heard it. That's why I know it was right. One fellow might have heard it, well you'd say, might imagine—but everybody heard it and everybody got up. And everything was the same way as we left them.

So I took the cards and I threw them in the stove. And we all went back to bed. And nothing happened. (*Did you ever play again?*) Not that way, not the kind of games we were playing. (*What kind of game?*) Well, it was this dirty talk and girls and boys, and how anyone could have such a mate, do such a thing.

145

Eddie: It wasn't gambling at all. But it wasn't proper. (*And do you think that was why you were hearing things?*) *Simon:* Well, I don't know. I couldn't see any other reason. Some people say you're not supposed to play cards on Sunday.... (*After that, did you change?*) Oh yes. I don't think I ever played that game since. And I never heard the cards since. *Eddie:* But this isn't a story that was made up at all. I was there too.

Simon: I'll tell you a story I heard. I suppose you heard it, it's so old. A fellow one time—a bunch of them playing cards—I guess they must have been gambling—anyhow, this side was losing, losing all. They couldn't win a game at all, at all. So a knock came to the door and this stranger came in and asked, could he play cards with them. They said, "Yes." He said he'd like to go on the side that was losing. So one fellow got up and he took his place. So they were then winning every game.

So one of the cards dropped on the floor. And one of the girls that was in the house, but wasn't playing, stooped down to pick up the card. And she noticed there was a clubbed foot on the stranger who had come in—a clubbed foot with a horse's hoof on it.

The girl went over and told somebody in the house that wasn't playing cards. The old fellow was supposed to be in bed, and he got up and he asked the stranger his name. He wouldn't tell them. So the old fellow went and got the Bible, and he started reading the Bible. And the stranger sprang from the table and jumped right up and went right up through the roof, put a hole right through it. And that was all that was ever seen of him.

And they could shingle it or do whatever they liked to that hole—they could never make it tight. Every time it would rain, it would leak.

That's an old, old story.

146

Dan Angus Beaton & the Dredge

I WAS NIGHT WATCHMAN on the Great
Lakes. Well, okay. On Sunday—in order to get
Sunday off, a day off, you had to work seven days
a week—the firemen, and watchmen. In order to
get a day off, on Sunday, you'd work the sixteen
hours. And that would give you a Sunday off.

So I was firing then. I was fireman. So, on
Sunday I'd have to go firing. And I'd stay the
sixteen hours and take the night watch, too. Get
me? The other fellow'd get the sixteen hours off.
And it was a steel hull, and the boiler and everything was down below. Big dredge.

Okay. This night I went out. This Jimmy Lacey—an awful fine man—he had a son a priest,
too. He'd be a man in his very early 60's, possibly. But those days, you didn't retire at 65. You
worked till 95 if you were capable of working.
But Jimmy was the most cowardly man I ever
saw in my life. All you had to say was mention a
ghost, and Jimmy was—oh, he was awful.

And Jimmy knew that I was a teetotal stranger,
that I didn't know anything about the rigs, I didn't
know anything about the area, anything about
anything. And he knew all about Dunbars (the
dredge company)—he was with them for years.

However, it was my turn. And I went on at
four o'clock, and I was to work through till seven
o'clock in the morning. And we were out seven
miles in the lake. Seven miles is what we were
out. And we had a rowboat. And we'd shut the
dynamos and everything off. Get me? So, we'd
have to put the lanterns out. But the fellow on
day was to have the lanterns all ready—he had

nothing else to do. So, all I'd have to do is light them and put them on the four corners, and put one on the steam gauge and one on the water glass, and so on.

So. I was sitting in the galley. She was equipped—had quarters on her for boarders at one time. But we were boarding ashore. I was sitting in the galley. And there was a good chair on her. I was sitting on the chair. And it was around, oh, in the evening, late in October—about this time, little later, late in October.

And—I heard somebody at the boiler—and everything fixed for the night, you know! You banked the—I don't know as if you know anything about the steam boiler or anything. But you bank it up and you fix it up for the night. Put enough water in it, put enough coal in it, to carry you over pretty near for the whole night. Do you understand? Fix it up for the night.

Well, I had it all fixed up. Nobody'd have to go near it till about morning. I was sitting down. Now, I'd not much more to do. I had the light all out, ready. It was lanterns we had. I had the dynamos all shut down. And, sit down. And God, I heard somebody shovelling coal down below. Was he ever shovelling coal! I was listening. And he was banging away with the old pan shovel, driving coal in the boiler. I jumped up, you know, and I was pretty cross. What business did anybody have putting coal in the boiler? I fixed the boiler up.

I got up, and I had my own lantern, the one that I carried. I grabbed the lantern, and I started down. When you'd get down below, it'd be dark. Up above was good enough—just dusk, you know—but when I'd get down below, it'd be dark. I grabbed the lantern, and down I went.

And I said, "What in hell are you interfering with my boiler for?" I said, "Whoever you are, stay the hell away from the boiler. I've got the boiler fixed for the night." I didn't know who it was. And I looked, and I pulled open the door and I looked. There wasn't a speck of coal put in it. I looked—the shovel was where I left it. I looked, and I couldn't see that anything was done. "Well," I said to myself, "holy sailors, what a fool. I was dead asleep, and I was dreaming. Hell," I said to myself, "I was dreaming, and I thought I was awake"—you know.

I looked, and sure enough, it's just suppertime. "I might as well have a lunch." And I started eating my lunch out of the can. Well, I was wide awake this time. I had a big thermos bottle, and eating a sandwich. The boy started shovelling again! Well, I'm awake this time! You know—no dream this time—I'm hearing him. Oh, the hearing was good then. And he was right under me. I listened. And I could almost count the shovelfuls that he was driving right into the boiler, you know. Oh, was he ever driving into the boiler!

I jumped up. And I was clear wild this time. Well, I'm damn sure he's putting coal in, you know. And I went down. Same result. No coal in the boiler. I went through, all around. Couldn't find anybody. "Well," I said to myself, "I'll know." I got a light, went right around the dredge. "If there's anybody around, he'd have to have a boat." 'Cause they were out seven miles. Not a boat, but mine. Nobody but me.

And then I went down and I examined. I said to myself, "If there's anybody aboard that stayed aboard." I hunted from top to bottom, and there wasn't anybody. And he couldn't leave without taking my boat. There was nobody.

Jimmy Lacey came the next morning. I asked him, "Jimmy, anybody ever get drowned or get killed around on this outfit?" "Why, why, why, Dan?"—you know, the first thing, you know—

"Why?" "Well," I said, "I'm asking you a question." "Why? Did you hear anything?" "Yes, I did." And I told him.

"Yes," he said. "This rig rolled over, going into Buffalo." He told me the year. "And," he said, "the cook and the fireman were both lost. I knew them both well. The cook and the fireman were drowned."

"Well," I said to him, "tell your son (the priest) that he's to have some masses and prayers said for that fireman," I said. "I heard him firing last night." "You'll never catch me on this rig alone! Never no more," he said. "You fellows can have her. But," he said, "I'll do what you said."

I never heard him after. (*You had a Mass said for him?*) Yeah. Never heard him after. I was aboard of it for years. I never heard him any more. I heard him just that one night. And I was aboard of her different times alone, and I never heard him since.

Catherine, Dan Angus's wife: He was just looking for a little help.

Dan Angus: He was just looking for a little help, I guess, the poor little fellow. (*You mean a mass.*) Yes.

Something very simple can keep you out of there. (*Out of where?*) Up above. *Catherine:* Out of Heaven. (*Apparently that's true.*) *Dan Angus:* This is true. You've got to know what it's all about.

"Father is haunting the house...."

I'VE TALKED TO MANY PEOPLE THAT SAID THAT THEY SAW THE DEAD PEOPLE. (*This is Bob Fitzgerald talking.*) Whether or not, whether or not it was just a figment of their imagination, I don't know. (*And you yourself...?*) I have never seen one. Personally, I don't believe in it.

But now, down home at White Point, our neighbour died. And his children, if they were living, will tell you that he haunted the house after he was dead. Gordon, his son, is dead and in his grave. Gordon told me he saw his father. And his daughter Florence, also dead and in her grave—the whole family is dead, for that matter. But I saw Gordon come to our house in the wintertime at eleven o'clock in the night—beautiful winter's night, not too much snow on the ground—calm, clear, nice, bright, moonlight winter's night, as bright as the day. And he came to my father's house—I was a young man then, eighteen years of age or something like that. And he was crying.

When he came in, my father asked him what was the trouble. And he said, "We want you to come down to the house." Father said, "What's the matter?" He said, "Florence saw Father. She's taken a turn." She was subject to epileptic turns, fits. So I said to Father, "I'll go down with you," and we went down.

I and my father went there, to that house, at eleven o'clock in the night. And when we went in, Willie—who was drowned in 19-and-43 or -44—he was walking the floor and he was crying. He was a young man then, twenty-eight or thirty I suppose, or something like that. He was walking the floor, and he was crying. And the other two children—Russell was the youngest—he was a young boy. I suppose he'd be eight or ten or twelve, or something like that. And he was in the rocking chair. His sister, Laura Mae, was rocking him. And she was older than him—she was fourteen or fifteen, I suppose. And they were crying. And their sister Florence was in a turn on the couch, lying on the couch. And she was in one of those epileptic fits or turns she used to take.

So we went in, I and my father. And Father said to Willie, "In the name of goodness gracious," he said, "Willie, what's the matter?" My father didn't believe in anything like that, you know, at all. And I can see Willie yet. He turned around and he was crying, and he said, "George, we have to do something." He said, "Father is driving us out of the house." He said, "Father is haunting the house."

Now, that was quite a thing, you know. It was right there, and to hear a man tell you that, a young man tell you that. And I was there—believe you me, I was there. I'm not making this up—I was there. And my father, you know, he didn't believe it. He said, "Oh, tut, tut," he said, "don't be so foolish."

So, I and my father went over where their sister Florence was on the couch. And we had seen her in many of those. And sometimes you'd have to hold a spoon in her mouth to keep her from chewing her tongue. So, after awhile she came to. And Father said, "What's your troubles?" She said, "George"—she always called Father George—that was his name. "George," she said, "I saw Father." And you know, Father wouldn't believe that kind of thing at all. And Father, ah, he brushed it off, said, "Oh, go on." She said, "No 'Go on' or 'Go away,' George." She said, "I know my father."

152

She said, "I went to that window"—now, it was a bright, beautiful moonlight night, as bright as the day. And where they sawed and split wood was right out by the side of the house. And she said, "I looked through the window, and there was a man standing by the splitting block there, with his foot up on the block. And," she said, "I went to the door. I thought it was Gus Dunphy" —one of their neighbours. She said, "I thought it was Gus. And," she said, "I went to the door."

Now, she was no distance from him; she was only six or eight feet from him. And she said, "I spoke to him and said, 'Come on in the house, Gus. What are you doing out here?' And he turned around and looked at me, George," she said, "and it was my father. Nobody else but my father."

Now, I listened to that. I was there. Whatever she saw, there was nobody else came in the house and there was nobody else there. She came in. She got that bad a fright that it put her into one of those epileptic fits that she used to take.

Now Gordon told me himself—he's dead and in his grave—Gordon told me himself that he saw his father. He said he saw him come up over the bank from the shore, and walk up to the house, and knock on the door, on the front door. (*And that was it.*) That was it.

(*Did they do anything to try to stop this?*) Yes, they did. I can tell you that, too. That noise, and that knocking, and that work around the house, and banging on, hammering around the house— kept it up till it finally drove them out of the house. In the summertime. One night in the summer. In 19-and-30. I was on the Great Lakes sailing when that happened. And they left the house. And the children left the house—Florence and Laura Mae and Russell left the house. And Gordon and Willie got in their motorboat and left for

Bay St. Lawrence where our parish priest was at, at that time.

And they left White Point at three o'clock in the morning, when they had to leave the house—they got in the boat and they left, and they went to Bay St. Lawrence, and they went to the glebe house. And they told the priest their troubles. And so, he listened to them, whatever it was or whatever it wasn't. And he told them to return back home, go back home. He said, "You won't be bothered any more."

And they went back home. And they were never bothered again.

WE WERE LATER TOLD by Cyril Dunphy, Gordon's son, that—as his father often told it—the noise that they heard was a loud banging against the outside of the house. No one but family saw or heard anything. And it was the priest's blessing of the house that put an end to these events.

Marguerite Gallant & Her Dreams

I'M NOT AFRAID OF MY DREAMS. Even if I would see someone who had died, so what?

I had a dream once that took all my fright. My mother had bought these prayer beads and a prayer book from an old lady. That was in Glace Bay. So she gave them to me. Great big long beautiful prayer beads. And after my mother died, my father had a cousin and she was a Sister and she gave him a crucifix—and I put this on the rosary bead.

One night—and I swear I was awake—and I swear this took all the fright I ever had in me and it never came back and I've never been afraid since—whether I was awake or sleeping I don't know. Anyway, I began to see by my bed two persons. And they were kneeling down. And they had veils over their face. And one had that prayer bead and one had the cross. And one said, "The beads are yours but the cross is mine." And I almost died.

But you don't die with fright. I learned that that night. And that's the only thing I have had in my life that didn't seem right.

So I took the prayer beads and the crucifix and I took a fork and I separated them. Then I went and told old Father LeBlanc. He said, "It might have been a dream and it might have been real." He said to give what the beads were worth. "I have no money," I said. He said, "Give what you have." So I gave 30 cents. He said, "Hang up the prayer beads." So I left the house for a time and left those beads still hanging on a nail. And they may be nailed up in the wall here to this day. Here somewhere. But I wouldn't want to find them.

I dreamed I saw Christ. He was so handsome. He had a beautiful grey gown. And he had something in his hand. I don't know what it was. And I was kneeling down by a little brook—the most beautiful brook; I wish that I could see it now—I could have touched Him. And there were the sweetest little ducks. And I was taking water like this in the cups of my hands and I was pouring on the duck's back. And I was so small. And yet I was so old. It was not so many many years ago. And yet I was so small, I was so little. Oh, the beautiful dreams I've had.

And after, I saw the Mother, the Blessed Virgin in the sky there. She had a halo of beautiful little white doves. There was, I would say, millions of them. And what a beautiful face. A little prettier than mine, I can tell you. And then I saw her again right at the end of Point Cross here. She was just hanging over the water, in a dream. The most beautiful thing I ever saw. She had on a grey old dress. They don't wear flashy colours.

I dreamt one night, I had a little boy in my arms. I was on a big battleship and it was all loaded with red roses. Then we were going through little portholes—and it didn't bother us any. We went through those little portholes so nicely. And all those beautiful roses. I never saw anything like it.

And you know what? When that boy actually died, he was twenty-one years old. And I was also alone with him. He was sick and I went there. I said, "I'm going home tomorrow." Rebecca said, "You go upstairs."

And I went upstairs and he was there. You know, a beautiful, handsome young man. Twenty-one years old. He said, "I'm so glad you came. You're going to stay with me until I get well." "Oh yes," I said, "I'll stay with you until you are well, if you don't take too long to get well. I have to go home." But I had to stay, that's all there was to it.

156

And he died on All Souls' Day. And he died in my arms. And it was during the war. And five minutes later, they had what they called a blackout. And I was kneeling by his bed and he had just died. Everybody flew out of the room and they left me there in the dark, and I was holding him still. And I believe that was my dream that I had so many years before. I was carrying him, not in my arm, *under* my arm, like that. I always carry things like that, under my arm.

You know, I don't dream a lot. But the other day I was telling a dream I had to Leo. He was over here. And he said, "Anyone who has a dream like that—they're lost. They're on the wrong road." Well, I guess he's right. But I don't think I ever had any bad dreams.

I dream of people that are gone certain times, but I'm not afraid of them. I'm not afraid of them when they're alive and I'm not afraid of them when they're dead.

Killing the Devil & Buying the Bull

THERE WAS A MAN I KNEW (*Donald John MacMullin told us*)—not myself. He was cutting coal out Port Morien—that's way out on the eastern coast of Cape Breton—and he was living down what we call here Sydney Forks. I saw the man. There were two or three of them. They were all pretty able but this fellow was pretty able anyhow. Fine looking man—big, red face. And they were seeing things down what they call Blackett's Lake Road.

I don't blame them for seeing things 'cause I was coming there with a horse and wagon when the cars came out a good many years ago. Car went straight instead of going around a turn and went into trees and there were two men killed. So, no doubt, they may have seen things.

But this man was walking home after working this day—walking home from Sydney—and he had a bottle of rum and he was taking a few drinks of rum. But at the Forks Bridge—Seven Mile Bridge we call it—he took a drink. He was scared of what was ahead of him. Foggy black night. You couldn't see a damn thing. But he was walking along, coming handy that little brook. That's where they used to see things.

And all of a sudden he heard a brrr-brrrrr, in the alders. He couldn't see nothing and he could hear the alders cracking. And that's all he heard, sort of a growl.

He said, "You're after frightening a lot here but you're not frightening me tonight." He said, "Come out where I'll get my hands on you."

So the thing was coming out.

He felt around and he could see nothing. But he found hair and small horns. Well, he thought he had the devil all right. And the thing pushed him, into his guts. And he came on with his fists and then he came on with the kicks and never quit till he figured he had killed the devil. Left him dead in the alders.

Early Sunday morning when most people would be walking up to East Bay, somebody called in. "Did you see down Allan MacMullin's— did you see the loss? They found their year-old black bull dead on the road."

He had to pay for the bull, but he killed the devil.

Art Severance Tells a Tale from Truthful Paul

WHEN I WAS STORM-STAYED Down North for three days, around 1928, we were over at the lobster factory. There was an old fellow lived handy there, known locally as Truthful Paul. And he could tell tall tales to no end. Well, I would say, just pure figments of the imagination. But very entertaining. That's all they were intended for. There was absolutely...there couldn't be any truth in them.

I remember one story he told there that really stuck with me. When he was a young fellow—a lot of men, of course, used to go to Maine in the winter, work in the lumber woods. And in the spring, they'd come back home. Well of course, Down North there in the spring, there still can be quite a bit of snow. So it was on one of these return trips coming home, I think he was supposed to be—this was himself, now, this Truthful Paul—this story was supposed to be something that happened to himself.

They'd be coming back to get ready for fishing in the spring. He had got down to Ingonish on a boat. He had to walk from there, going home. Going north.

So anyway, somewhere down between Ingonish and Neil's Harbour, I think it would be, what they call the Broad Cove Mountain—it was getting kind of late. And he said the travelling, the walking was bad. He had got into the heavy snow. He was getting pretty tired, and he was wishing that he could find a house somewhere along the way to call in and spend the night. Anyway, he said he was tramping along, and he was getting weary, and his steps were getting shorter and harder and slower.

Suddenly he heard singing—Gaelic songs, of course. Well, he said that put a little bit more life into him. He knew there was something. So he just tried to get along faster. And sure enough, he said, he caught up with this bunch of young people, and they were heading for a house. There was to be a milling frolic at this house.

So they got to the house. And of course, he wasn't there very long when he had a cup of tea and something to eat, and felt a lot better, he said, and was sitting there. The milling got under way. By and by, there was some noise at the door, and the man of the house went to the door. "Ah well, Rory," he said, "you're not very early tonight, but you're early enough." He said, "They're still milling."

This great big man with a big long white beard right down to his waist, carrying a bundle. It was just wrapped up in a shawl, and he had that under his arm. He came in, and this old lady came in behind him. And she had a spinning wheel on her shoulder, and a pair of wool cards hung on a cord at her waist. So they came in and sat down. Oh, they got a cup of tea for the old couple right quickly.

Anyway, after they had the tea, the milling was pretty nearly finished. The old man turned to the old lady, said, "Morag, it's time to get to work." Well, the old lady got up and left. By golly, when she went out, when she took the wool cards off the cord, there was a pair of wool shears there, too. She went out and she took the shears. After a little while she came back in, and she had this handful of wool. She sat down with the wool cards, and she started carding the wool and making rolls. She got the rolls made. She started the spinning wheel going.

The old man said to her, "Well now, Morag, do the fine ones first." Well, he said, she spun threads that were just like spider webs, they were that thin. And she spun them, and they'd be about that long, and she'd hang them over the back of the chair, till at last she had a bunch there, he said, was just about hardly as big around as your little finger.

After these little ones were all spun, the old man told one of the young fellows to go out—I don't know what kind of a wood it was, he didn't name it—to cut a switch. And he'd have to cut it so long, he told him. So the young fellow went out, anyway, and he got this switch and he brought it in. And while he was getting the switch, Rory told her, told the old lady, "Now, Morag," he said, "do the E string first."

So, she spun the four strings for the fiddle that he had. But, he said, he'd never seen a fiddle like it. When the old man unwrapped this parcel that was done up with the plaid blanket, it looked more like a big bottle. He put the strings on that, anyway. And he took the switch. He measured off so long—and he made a notch in either end of the switch. Took these little threads that she had spun first, took them all up, made a knot in one end, and stripped them all out to get them even, and then made a knot in the other end. Bent the switch into a bow, put it through the threads, let the ends go and the threads hooked in the notch at either end of the switch. That was the bow.

Well, he said, the old man tuned the fiddle and he started to play. And the young folks, he said, they were all on the floor then to dance. The milling was finished, of course.

Well, he said, he had never danced in his life. But whatever was in that music, he said, he didn't know, because he couldn't dance. But whatever was in that music, he was surprised to find himself on the floor, dancing. And for weeks afterwards, he said, he'd wake up in the middle of the night, out of bed on the floor, dancing. He said that music would be ringing in his ears. He'd never heard anything like it.

Anyway, coming about daylight, and the strings were just disintegrated on the fiddle, and that was the end of the dance. And the bow, too, they were just worn out.

So they were all leaving, they were all going. Morag and Rory had gathered up their cards and their shears and got the spinning wheel on her shoulder, and they were going out. The crowd had all left, anyway. He waited till all the rest were gone. He wanted to thank his hosts for their hospitality and so on. After doing this, he started out.

When he went out, he said, there was Morag and Rory. There was a little garden fence, and there was a ram tied to the fence. Rory was just untying the ram off the corner of the fence. And he was all sheared, he said, except one little patch on one hip. And when he was going down the road, he heard Rory telling Morag there was just enough wool on the ram for one more dance.

ALSO AVAILABLE FROM Breton Books

The Cape Breton Giant
by James D. Gillis
with "A Memoir of Gillis" by Thomas H. Raddall
$8.00

Down North:
The Original Book of Cape Breton's Magazine
Word-and-Photo Portrait of Cape Breton • 239 pages, 286 photographs
$22.35

Cape Breton Lives:
A Second Book from Cape Breton's Magazine
300 pages of Life Stories, 120 photographs
$22.35

Castaway on Cape Breton:
Ensign Prenties' *Narrative* of Shipwreck at Margaree Harbour, 1780
Edited with an Historical Setting and Notes by G. G. Campbell
TO WHICH IS ADDED
Samuel Burrows' *Narrative* of Shipwreck on the Cheticamp Coast, 1823
With Notes on Acadians Who Cared for the Survivors by Charles D. Roach
$11.25

Highland Settler
A Portrait of the Scottish Gael in Cape Breton and Eastern Nova Scotia
by Charles W. Dunn
"This is one of the best books yet written on the culture of the Gaels of Cape
Breton and one of the few good studies of a folk-culture." *Western Folklore*
$14.25

Cape Breton Music Cassettes:

Mike MacDougall's Tape for Fr. Hector
60 minutes of terrific Cape Breton fiddle music, newly re-mastered
$10.00

Cape Breton Fiddlers on Early LPs:
Dan R. MacDonald • Theresa MacLellan
Dan Joe MacInnis • Donald MacLellan • Johnny Wilmot
A great introduction to Cape Breton Music.
$10.00

Winston "Scotty" Fitzgerald: House Parties and 78s
90 minutes of music!
$11.25

Breton Books & Tapes
Wreck Cove, Nova Scotia B0C 1H0
PRICES INCLUDE GST AND POSTAGE